"100% YES! skilfully guides you in releasing what's been holding you back so you can be free to embrace the success you desire. If you are interested in accessing the powerful inner state that allows you to become unstoppable and sets you up to achieve your goals, read this book and apply its powerful techniques."

— **Jack Canfield**
Bestselling Co-author of The Success Principles™, Tapping into Ultimate Success and the Chicken Soup for the Soul series

"100% Yes is filled with gems of wisdom mixed with practical tools to help you take the next step. Steve has a gift in showing the reader how to identify conscious and unconscious blocks and how to break free. This isn't a book you simply read; it's a transformational experience."

— **Jessica Ortner**
NY Times Bestselling Author of The Tapping Solution for Weight Loss and Body Confidence

"Even the most successful people struggle with parts of their lives that just don't seem to fall into line. In this book Steve Wells shows how to align with success 100%, a state in which no part of your being is objecting to success. If you're looking for an approach to resolve those parts of your life that, despite your best efforts, still aren't marching in tune with your highest aspirations, this book is for you."

—**Dawson Church**
PhD Best-selling author of The Genie in Your Genes

"If you are serious about being the most successful, fulfilled and happy person you can be then you need to read and re-read this insightful and fabulous book. We all have invisible inhibitors that stop us being the best we can be and by discovering these and working on them yourself, in your own home, you can really start to fly - NOW!"

— **Maggie Dent**
Australian author, parenting and resilience specialist

"Steve Wells' life-changing work on emotional alignment, values and goals shows how an author's depth, insight and experience make for excellent reading and a deeply accessible and practical book. I highly recommend you let Steve Wells guide you to live in your 100% YES! Success State - it will be totally worth the journey!"

— **Carol Look**

Founding EFT Master, Author of Attracting Abundance with EFT,
Creator of "The Yes Code"

"100% Yes! is a fantastic resource for anyone who is ready to stop simply dreaming of the life they want and actually make it happen. As you follow along with numerous real life examples, you will gain greater clarity about what you really want, and clear out the internal objections that have kept it out of reach. Using Steve's process, success becomes natural."

— **Brad Yates**

EFT Expert, Co-author of Freedom at Your Fingertips

"100% YES! is a clear guide with powerful tools and practical steps to help you clarify and achieve your own unique version of success. Steve's structured approach to get clear on values helps us understand what's actually holding us back and gives us clear ways to overcome it. Even with my 10 years+ of tapping to help people in the arena of success, there were new, powerful tools here that I'm excited to use."

— **Pamela Bruner**

Business Coach, Co-author, Tapping into Ultimate Success

"Steve Wells is a pioneer and master in the therapeutic uses of acupoint tapping. In 100% YES! he has synthesized his decades of experience into the simplest and most user-friendly self-help format he could envision. But don't be fooled. This book can guide you in confronting inner barriers to success, outmoded beliefs, and conflicts in your goals as you move forward toward a life that is inspired by your highest possibilities."

— **David Feinstein**

Ph.D. Co-author, The Promise of Energy Psychology and The Energies of Love

"Beginning with clean and inspiring definitions of success, Steve Wells offers expert guidance in harnessing the power of commitment, decision, resolving values conflicts, and goal setting. An essential centrepiece is SET, his Energy Psychology tools that guarantee success. We witness and learn from Steve's expert skill as we eavesdrop on his provocative and powerful work with participants in workshops. Read, experience, and apply what you'll learn from this user friendly book."

— **Fred P. Gallo**
PhD. Author of Energy Psychology and President of the Association for
Comprehensive Energy Psychology

"Steve's work with values is transformational ... His gift is his ability to identify the conflicts (both conscious and unconscious) that interfere with us achieving our goals and fully engaging in our lives in a purposeful authentic way. By gently challenging and questioning ourselves, following the techniques in this book, Steve offers us the opportunity to create a life which is more fulfilling and peaceful, and in alignment with our truth. This book is written with clarity and insight and is easy to follow and Steve's compassion and therapeutic experience shine through every page."

— **Emma Roberts**
EFT Master, Co-author of Step by Step Tapping

"Steve Wells nails the problem most people face, they don't have a clear understanding of what success is to them personally. Success and achievement without first getting clarity about your values will leave you exhausted, unsatisfied, and not able to realize your dreams. 100% YES! not only gives you the roadmap for gaining a true sense of where to go, but also gives you a step-by-step process for doing it through exercises and simple processes. I will enthusiastically share this book with my clients and students."

— **Alina Frank**
EFT and Matrix Reimprinting Trainer, and Best Selling Author of How to
Want Sex Again Using EFT

"In this book Steve Wells explores success as an inside job and offers fabulous tools and insights to help every reader find their way to unleashing their own mojo and create the life dreams that we all so richly deserve. A great resource for ANYONE looking to make their life an exciting adventure even as their dreams are still being constructed and manifested."

— Craig Weiner

DC, EFT and Matrix Reimprinting Trainer

"A powerful book on success, energy healing and living your full potential with pearls of wisdom throughout. Steve shows us how to use his (and colleague Dr. David Lake's) signature SET Technique to elegantly clear blocks, which naturally leads to embracing our most important values, beliefs and goals to reach a 100% YES! with our lives."

— Phillip Mountrose

Co-author of Getting Thru to Your Emotions with EFT

"Steve Wells' 100% YES! can help you turn your life around. The newly emerging strategies explained in this book embrace innovative techniques which take you deep into your unconscious to uncover the root of your negative programming, not just skim the surface. Steve shows us how to use these powerful tools in new ways to accelerate results and empower us beyond anything you may have previously believed was possible."

— Sharon Cass-Toole

PhD, DCEP, Executive Director, Canadian Association for Integrative and Energy Therapies (CAIET)

100% YES!

The Energy of Success

Release your Resistance
Align your Values
Go for your Goals

Using Simple Energy Techniques (SET)

By Steve Wells

Waterford Publishing

ISBN-13: 978-0-9579386-3-2
ISBN-10: 0-9579386-3-2

Edited by: Anita Saunders, Cindy Barrilleaux
Formatting: Leila Summers
Cover Design © Shaan Coutinho

This book is for educational and informational purposes only. The author does not dispense medical advice or prescribe the use of any technique as a form of treatment for physical or mental problems without the advice of a physician or mental health professional, either directly or indirectly. The intent of the author is only to offer information of a general nature to help you in your quest for emotional and spiritual well-being.

The author and/or publisher do not guarantee that anyone following the techniques, suggestions, tips, ideas, or strategies in this book will become successful. This also applies to transcribed demonstrations: results achieved are illustrations only and cannot be guaranteed for others.

While in practice the outcomes of using Simple Energy Techniques (SET), or "tapping" are positive for many people, this may not apply to you in full or to your particular problem or issue. As tapping is not yet widely accepted as a formally validated scientific technique it must be considered experimental in nature with no guaranteed outcome in any individual. In the event that you use any of the information in this book for yourself, which is your constitutional right, the author and publisher assume no responsibility for your actions.

Waterford Publishing
PO Box 54, Inglewood, Western Australia, 6932

Printed in the United States of America

DEDICATION

To my darling wife Louise

From the moment our eyes first met, you have been my 100% YES!

CONTENTS

INTRODUCTION

I wrote this book because I want to show how to break through the barriers that are currently preventing you from having the success and living the life that you desire. I want you to know that no matter what your current situation, you can turn your life around. I know this from my own personal experience and that of many thousands of clients and workshop participants who have learned and applied these powerful techniques. You too can see them transform your life.

Recent exciting discoveries in the world of psychology and self-development have led to powerful new methods for personal change that can help you get where you want to go more rapidly and with less stress than ever before. These techniques, from the emerging field of Energy Psychology, are nothing less than revolutionary.

Techniques such as Emotional Freedom Techniques (EFT) and Simple Energy Techniques (SET) aka "tapping" have the potential to help you become free from the limiting effects of negative emotions in your life, emotions that may have been preventing you from achieving the success you desire.

"Happiness is when what you think, what you say, and what you do are in harmony." — Mahatma Gandhi

My aim in this book is to show you how to use these techniques to free yourself from emotional blocks that are behind self-sabotage, procrastination, inertia and false starts. Then you can be free to go for your goals 100%. In what I call '100% YES!', no parts of you are holding back, and the feeling that the wind is at your back replaces that sense of constantly pushing against resistance. I am going to show you how to use these powerful tools in new ways to accelerate your results beyond anything you may have previously believed was possible.

What is 100% YES! ?

100% YES! is a state in which your energy flows naturally, you ride the horse in the direction it's going and you don't have to work against your own energy to be successful. Every part of you is working towards the same end because you know that **this is what you really want** and that **it is going to be good for you on all levels**. To get there, you may need to confront and break through limiting beliefs, realign your values and clarify your own vision of success. The tools taught in this book will help you to do that.

How to use this book

This book is designed to be part guidebook, part workbook, and part workshop *experience*. I designed it to help you to progress step by step through the process of learning and *applying* these powerful techniques to achieve your own freedom. I also want to inspire you with examples of what is possible using these techniques so I've included extensive transcribed demonstrations of real people working on real issues from my live 100% YES! Workshops (All used with permission, many are composites, and names have been changed). I want this to feel a bit like a workshop in a book, to capture some of the energy and inspiration of the live workshop experience. Finally, it's a guidebook on how to access your power to create and live your life your way. My fondest hope is that you will not only read this book, but that you will use the techniques taught herein to help you make the changes you seek, to uncover and live your 100% YES!

Let's go!

Success Begins With a Decision

Your power to decide may be the greatest power you have. Everything that you do starts with a decision. So right now I invite you to decide that you are going to make the changes you want, achieve the goals you want, and improve your life in the ways you want, and that you will use the material in this book to help you get there.

This book provides you with many ideas and strategies that have been proven by others to be effective. However, ultimately it's your decisions about what to do with it that will make the biggest difference in your life.

If you use the techniques and follow through on the exercises in this book, then I'm confident that you will be heading for a dramatically different life than the one you had before you opened these pages.

Using the Techniques

Before we go any further, I need to caution you against limiting the ways you use the techniques you are about to learn. Many people who learn these tools tend to use them only on a surface level when they really could be using them on a much deeper level. For example, you can use the techniques to overcome a fear or phobia, yet underneath that you may still have negative beliefs that underlie that fear. It is a great thing to become free of something that used to upset you, but this is a 'remedial' focus, aimed at fixing problems. However, there is much more that you can do than just use these techniques to simply relieve a problem feeling or overcome a current limitation. Releasing your attachments to underlying negative beliefs is a deeper level of work that will take you much further.

For example, let's say you have a fear of flying, so you use one of the techniques in this book to overcome that fear so that now you are able to fly without fear. And you feel really good about yourself for wiping out the fear. Well, that's great, but if you have an underlying belief that you are not a good person, then a week later another reason to be upset with yourself will pop up. Sure, you can fly now, but at a deeper level, you still hold the belief that YOU are unworthy. You can overcome those inner negative beliefs with these techniques, which allows you to live your highest ideals. That's the reason I caution you not to miss out on the powerful effects of applying the techniques to overarching issues as well as surface problems.

Reset Your Inner Command System

I'm interested in helping you to deal with this underneath part, the 'stuff' you take with you everywhere—your beliefs about yourself and *how you feel about yourself.* We can call this your inner 'central command system'. It consists of your beliefs about yourself, about the world, about what's possible for you, your life, your career, your family and much, much more. These beliefs greatly influence where you're going to go in life and what you're going to do. They both define and limit your experience of life.

If you change just one of your core beliefs, you can change a whole area of your life. If you use these techniques to go even further to change your *core identity beliefs*—your beliefs about who you think you are and what is possible for you—***then your whole life*** changes. That is the sort of change I am interested in—change at a core level—and that is the main subject of this book.

If you apply what you learn in this book, by the end of it you will find that you haven't just made a small difference in your life, your whole life will be better. You will be happier with yourself and more empowered to live the life you really want to live.

The book provides exercises that enable you to achieve that goal. So be sure to complete the exercises throughout the book, rather than just reading them. They will help you more clearly define what you *really* want out of life and how to get it. You may think you already know what you want out of life, and perhaps you do. However, it wouldn't be surprising if, like many people, you are living your life according to old 'programs' and scripts that are out of date and no longer relevant to who you are now. The exercises will help shake up some of those old programs and ultimately help you to release them. You'll get underneath what you think you want and discover what you *really* want *now*. When you identify what I call your true values and make them the focus of your life, you'll find it easier to get what you want *and* you'll want what you get. Your overall happiness will soar.

So, right now, think about what you want to get from this book. And decide, right now, that you are going to do the exercises so you can get what you want. It's my experience that you will be surprised to not only get what you want, but *even more*.

CHAPTER 1

The Twin Decisions of Success

I believe in order to be truly successful, there are two decisions you need to make. The first is to decide what success is to you. But that is not enough to take you there. Then you have to decide to have it, to make it real.

Let me repeat that so it's clear: There are two decisions to make. *First,* decide what you want *then* decide to make it real. Lots of people do the first part but never go so far as to do the second part, and that is why they aren't successful.

You have to develop a vision of success that inspires *you*, not someone else's vision. Too many people are running on other people's visions of success. Someone once said you can spend your entire life climbing the ladder of success and then get to the top of the ladder and realise it's been leaning against the wrong wall. What a tragedy. This is what I want to help you to avoid.

In searching for what success really is for you, we are going to focus not only on the goals you want to achieve but also on the things that are most important to you *underneath* your goals. *What do you really want out of those goals?*

So let's get started. Write down your answers to the following questions:

What is success *to you*? أنا وكذلك نفسي

What is *your version* of success?

What is your *ultimate* vision of success? Inspire people

I've been running my business for 20 years now. Back when I first started my business and for probably the first four or five years the thought kept coming to me that I wasn't running a real business, even though I was quite successful. One day I suddenly woke up and realised, *I don't have to run my business the way everyone else does. I can create and run my business how I want, to do whatever I want, to build the life that I want. I don't have to live someone else's life.*

And so whilst I have learnt from others I have ultimately developed my own version of business success, a business that fulfils my lifestyle goals and makes a difference in the world at the same time.

So, what is success *to you*?

Have you written down your answers to that question? If not, take the time and do it now.

Here are some sample versions of success brought up by participants in my 100% YES! workshops:

- *Being able to choose without financial considerations.*

- *Having the freedom to do what I want, when I want it, where I want it, how I want it.*

- *Success to me is inner peace and joy in my heart.*

- *I want to be financially independent and I want to be authentic. Being real so that I'm not trying to live according to other people's expectations of me. "I am who I am and that's the way I am."*

- *To be totally comfortable and accepting of myself regardless of the opinions of others.*

- *Number one, I want to spend lots of quality time with my family. Number two, to choose how I spend my time. Number three, to meet interesting people. Number four, to spread joy, making a difference in people's lives. Number five, to leave a legacy through a body of work. Number six, to laugh and have fun every day.*

- *Spending my time with people I like and love. Another is having financial freedom, which is my main challenge at the moment. Removing that barrier which can sometimes impede on the things you already have that you're not necessarily showing much appreciation for.*

- *Having time and money, not one at the expense of the other.*

- *Having freedom to choose where we live, where we go on holiday and what work I might do or not do, and contributing to others generously.*

Here are three of my favourite definitions of success:

1. *"Success is the progressive realization of a worthy goal."* — Earl Nightingale

A lot of people see success as only being the achievement of the goal. The problem with that is that you don't get to feel happy until you've achieved your goal, you don't get to celebrate anything along the way, and you don't get to be happy with something great which is not quite what you initially envisaged. Then once you have achieved that goal, what do you do? Now you have to set another goal. So you never get to feel successful.

In Earl Nightingale's definition, which I really like, it's the progressive realisation of a goal that is worthy of you, which is success. It's having something to live for, having something to work for, having something to move you, having a reason to get up in the morning, and, if it's inspiring enough, something to keep you up late.

2. *"Success is creating a state of mind that allows you to do whatever it is you really want."* — Mark Victor Hansen and Robert Allen, *The One Minute Millionaire.*

I love this definition! That's very close to what I would call a '100% YES!' state, where you can go for it 100%, you're unimpeded, you don't have to be held back by fear or negative beliefs.

These authors are expert at getting into the state that they believe is essential to their success and they have both been very successful. And that state allowed them to go through quite some obstacles to get there. As one example, Mark and his original business partner Jack Canfield had a great idea to publish a compilation of inspiring stories they'd gathered from their friends and peers. They submitted their manuscript to 33 publishers and not one wanted to publish it. So they went to a book fair and

10

ended up putting it in front of a total of 105 different publishers. All of them rejected it until someone finally did accept it.

Jack and Mark have now sold over 500 million copies of the *Chicken Soup for the Soul* series, with over 200 titles in the series. They created a publishing empire.

I think the 104 publishers who rejected them have probably all jumped off a bridge, or thought about it. When they were assessing the book they should have paid attention to the people who were presenting it to them. If they'd been able to perceive the *state the authors were in*, they'd have known it was going to be successful, because the promotion the authors are willing to do is a huge part of the success of any book. However, they couldn't make a true assessment because they were just looking at something on paper.

Mark Victor Hansen and Robert Allen used a similar approach to pre-sell a million copies of *The One Minute Millionaire*. It didn't just happen by chance. *They decided they wanted to achieve that.* Then they got a bunch of people in the room and paid them $70,000 to brainstorm ideas for pre-selling a million books. The whole time they were focused on being in a state of believing it was going to happen. Then they acted on the key ideas that came forth and lo and behold their desired result was achieved.

3. *"Success is something you attract by the person you become."* — Jim Rohn

To be successful, focus on developing yourself, and becoming the type of person who can be that successful. Change your own attractive power and you're automatically attracted towards those things that will work for you—and other people who can help you get there will also be attracted towards you.

Power is an Inside Job

Quite a few years ago I worked with the state men and women's touch rugby teams in my home state of Western Australia. At one point I was talking with the men's team about their goals. I said to the group, *Someone tell me one of your goals.* A big guy called out, *I want a 1100 cc motorbike.* I replied, *Okay, if you have that 1100 cc motorbike what's that going to give you?* He said, *Power!*

He wants to be powerful. He wants to feel like a powerful person. And he thinks if he gets a motorbike, he will *be* powerful. He's made the connection (some people would say he's given away his own power) that power is going to come from something outside of him. It's actually a false connection but people do this all the time.

Once he gets the motorbike, he might decide, *Because I've got a powerful motorbike it means I'm a more powerful person,* and now he gives himself permission to feel powerful inside.

I see this as being like the Wizard of Oz who turned out to be just an ordinary person and when he realised he had been found out still uttered the words, *Never mind the man behind the curtain. I am the Wizard of Oz!* It was all a facade. But we do this all the time. You believe you are now a powerful person because you are wearing a powerful person's clothes. You are brave because you have a medal. You are smart because you have a diploma. But it isn't necessarily so.

If you haven't changed yourself inside, you can have the powerful motorbike and the right clothes and the muscular body, and all the other trappings of so-called power, yet still feel like a weakling inside.

Some years ago I saw an arts festival film called *Leolo*. I thought it was an absolutely awful film, but I watched it all the way through because I was trying to get some culture. There were all sorts of weird imagery and allusions throughout the film, some of which I struggled to understand. But there was one section in the film which had a powerful effect on me, and this was a segment focusing on Leolo's older brother.

When the two boys rode their bikes into town the town bully would invariably come along and push Leolo's brother off his bike. This happened every single time. One day this guy reads a magazine with the Charles Atlas advertisement on the back cover where the weakling develops himself into a strong man and no longer gets sand kicked in his face. So he decides he's going to become a big, strong man and sends away for the muscle-building equipment. He gets the equipment, does the exercises, builds up his muscles and eventually he becomes really bulked up.

Later in the film Leolo and his brother ride their bikes into the town and the town bully walks up to them. The brother takes off his shirt and flexes his muscles, which are quite impressive. The town bully takes one look at him, sneers, laughs, and pushes him over anyway! He's lying there crying in the gutter, and watching this I had the thought: *He's changed on the outside but he hasn't changed how he feels inside. He never found the power inside himself to really become a stronger person.*

That's what we're really after: creating that shift *inside*.

I hope you understand that if you are able to find the power inside yourself you will never need to buy a big motorbike to prove you are powerful. Any time you want, you'll be able to access that powerful feeling inside you. And if you do want the motorbike, you can still have it! In fact, if you can easily access your own power, you'll be able to obtain that motorbike much more easily, and enjoy it much more than someone who feels weak inside and is desperately wanting it to prove they are powerful (all the while feeling like they are not).

CHAPTER 2

Expanding Your Version of Success

Let's look at your version of success for a moment. You wrote it down earlier, right? Well, I have news for you ...

Your current version of success probably sucks!

If you are like many people I've asked to define success, there is a good chance that your current version of success is not helping you to succeed and may even be preventing you from succeeding...

You see, if your version of success was so great then either you would be successful right now, or at the very least you would be going for it 100%, without holding back, and you wouldn't need to read this book.

So what do I mean when I say that your version of success may suck, and what is the secret to creating a version of success that doesn't suck?

There are a couple of common ways that I've found that people's versions of success tend to suck!

Your version of success sucks if ...

1. It is constricted

Your version of success almost certainly isn't as expansive as it could be. Most people are holding themselves back due to fear and blocking beliefs, which keep their vision smaller than it could be. If this is you then you'll benefit from learning the techniques in this book to release your blocking beliefs and overcome your fear, then you'll be able to see further and go further.

2. It is conflicted

Most people see their big life goals as an 'either-or' situation, a conflict between two or more possibilities. For example, once I asked a gentleman, *What would happen if you were successful?* He said, *If I was successful I'd lose my marriage.*

I said, *That doesn't sound like success to me because either way you lose. If you want to keep your marriage then why don't you keep that in your version of success? Why doesn't your version of success enable you to be successful* **and** *married?*

In his version of success it's one or the other. You can't have both. Therefore he's got to endure a constant fight between two parts of himself, between the part that wants to be successful in business and the part that wants to have a happy marriage. He doesn't see a way that he can have both, so he is stuck with having to decide between them. Instead of win-win his version is lose-lose. And this is a recipe for procrastination, false starts, inertia and, ultimately, misery.

For most people, their version of success is conflicted like this, which means that it excludes important parts of their life. So it is like they are saying, *Okay, I can get that but if I do I'm going to lose this* or *If I get what I want over here, I'm going to miss out on something that's important to me over there.* It's either-or.

A very common example, and one which I suffered from, is the belief *If I am successful at work it means I won't be there for my family* or *If I am there for my family I have to give up my goals of achieving or making a difference in the world.*

This kind of belief conflict where if one side wins the other loses means ultimately that because you really want *both* of them then part of you has to lose in order for the other part to win. That's not success, not from where I sit. For one thing, it focuses you on loss rather than gain. And how can you feel successful if part of you has to lose?

This comes up in particular when people talk about their weight: they always tend to focus on weight *loss*. It's a negative focus. When they talk about diets they're focusing on the first three letters: die! It's deprivation time, it's missing-out time. It means you're not allowed to have any fun anymore. *How on earth are you going to be motivated to not have any fun?*

Now your goal is *Okay, I'm going to be successful. Success equals pain. Let's go and have some more pain!* Well, that's not going to motivate you, is it? That version of success is simply not going to work.

I don't care how wonderful your version of success is, there's got to be part of you holding back otherwise you would be there right now. There's got to be part of you that thinks, the process of getting there is going to be difficult for me. It's going to require something that I don't have. It's going to require me to do stuff that I don't want to do. When I get there it's not actually going to be that good. It's going to put more pressure on me. One or another of these kinds of thoughts—these kinds of beliefs—is in your way of having the success you desire, otherwise you'd be going for it 100%.

The 100% YES! State

I believe there's a state that we access at various times in our lives which I call 100% YES! It is a state where your energy is in flow, where no part of you is holding back. You ride the horse in the direction it's going and when you find something to do you do it with all your might. It's a state where you know that what you are doing is good: good for you, good for other people, good for the planet. Every part of you is working towards the same end. You are in alignment.

The challenge is that often when we think about success or think about our goals, we think it'll be good, and there will also be something which is bad. Therefore we have an inner conflict. If we can't iron out that conflict, we exhaust ourselves fighting against part of us that wants to do this, and part of us that doesn't want to do it. We're pushed and pulled in all kinds of directions by our own internal programs, many of which are unconscious to us.

Winston Churchill called this internal civil war. It's where you want this *and* you want that. Comedian Steven Wright says, *You can't have everything, where would you put it?* Some people say in response, *Well give me a chance, I'll try and find out.*

The reality, however, is you don't want *everything* in the world. There are some things you do want and some things you don't want. And not all of the things you want are equal, some you want more than others. Some are more important than others. And some things you think you want are not what you really want; what you really want is what you think those things are going to give you.

The best way to go is to first identify what it is that you *really* want, then focus on getting the barriers out of the way to be able to have that and do that and be that. I'm interested here in the goals that you have where maybe you think something like, *I would love to do this. But I feel like I'm not good enough or I feel like maybe it will be too hard for me.*

The work you do on overcoming those belief barriers allows us to manifest parts of you which really need to be in the world. Joseph Campbell would say find out who you really are and bring that out into the world.

Ultimately this process is not so much about putting something *in* to us to make us good enough. It's about taking stuff away. What we're talking about is stripping away a lot of the internal gunk which is in the way of our being able to see what we need to do and what we *really* want and what's really right for us.

Where we're heading, the direction forward, is accessing and spending more time in *your 100% YES! state, the state where your energy flows.*

When you are driven by that success state, work doesn't feel like work, work becomes worthwhile. And it's like the things you want are simultaneously attracted toward you.

"What you seek is seeking you." — *Rumi*

Ultimately what we're after is getting into that success state and living there more of the time. That means you get to *feel successful* more of the time. Many people say you can't do that because if you feel successful then you won't be motivated to achieve more. The belief is *I have to achieve in order to be happy and if I'm happy then I will stop achieving.* Well, that's not true at all. The reality is if you have to make yourself feel bad in order to achieve not only is that demotivating and energy sapping, it becomes the state in which you spend most of your time (i.e. frustration, anger or misery). It's the opposite of success. Conversely, if you are in a success state you are energised and motivated and you feel happy to keep on working and achieving; you have plenty of energy for it.

So, that's what we're working towards. Obviously that's not a state we are going to be in all the time because life goes through cycles and there are various barriers that prevent us from being successful. Breaking through those barriers and releasing any emotional blocks to succeeding is our greatest challenge.

CHAPTER 3

Breaking Through the Barriers – Achieving 100% YES!

If you have done the exercise earlier in this book and written down your version of success, the question I have for you is *Why aren't you successful right now?*

*What are the **barriers** that are in your way that prevent you from being that, doing that or having that right now?*

Write down your answers to these questions because that's what we're going to work on next. These questions identify some of your blocking beliefs which may previously have been unconscious until you started to consider making a change and moving up to a new level of success.

Just for now write down some of the things that you believe are in the way for you.

*What **prevents you** from being successful right now?*

We are going to come back to the answers to these questions later and do some work on these beliefs to help you overcome them and release them for good.

Overcoming Your False Associations and Beliefs About Success

I have a lot of respect for this quote from Anthony Robbins:

For everything you want, the only reason you don't have it is because you associate more pain than pleasure to what it would take to have it.

That means on some level you associate that there is going to be pain involved in *the process of becoming* successful, or there's going to be pain associated with *being* successful (or both). If that *wasn't* the case, then surely you would be going for it, 100%.

So, for example, you may associate, *If I have a lot of money then I'll have to work so hard that I won't get to see my family and then I'll lose them and be lonely* or *If I have a lot of money then I'll become a greedy, unspiritual person.* Negative associations like this are often what is really holding many people back from taking definite action towards their goals and dreams.

When you think about being successful in the ways you want, what feeling does it give you? If it gives you a yucky inner feeling to think about doing it, then it is like connecting this thought to taking action: *Let's go have some more yuck feeling!* That's not really going to motivate you, is it? You're not going to move towards something which gives you a repulsion effect. So, in fact, many of your goals have both an attractive force and a repulsive force at the same time: a yes and a no.

This is the opposite of all spiritual philosophy that works well.

There's a Buddhistic injunction that says sit or stand, don't oscillate. In the Bible in the book of Revelation it says be definite, be hot or cold, don't be lukewarm. Make your yes, **yes** and your no, **no**.

The challenge comes when you have the yes and no mixed up in your version of success. When we are stuck within this pattern of either-or thinking, we can't see that there's a way of having it all work together. A common conflict here is between family and career. Now I do believe there's usually an order and sequence to what we want and we do have to respect that, so for example family may be more important than career to you or vice versa. But ultimately, all parts work together, and you *can* have both.

What we want is to find that balance where all of the things we really want can work together, so that achieving each helps the others. That to me is 100% YES!

100% YES! isn't about finding one thing that's important to you and saying, "Okay, I'm 100% career or 100% family." I'm sure most kids wouldn't really like their parents to be with them every minute of every day! It's more about finding a way that your values can work together *for you*. So, for example, success in your career feeds your family, supports your family, and inspires your kids, and success in your family provides the foundation and energy for success in your career.

100% YES! is about living your unique combination of values in a way that most serves you, makes you happy and also serves the world.

Before you can create your success picture you've got to believe you can have all of the things you *really* want, rather than just some of them, and to understand that success isn't win-lose or lose-lose but can be win-win and even win-win-win-win-win.

To do this, you'll need to release any negative beliefs which say you can't have this *and* that. There is a way of having both, you just need to discover it for yourself. Yes, it will be true that one is more important than another. But you don't have to totally give up one for the other, you just need to get the order and sequence right *for you*.

A Personal Example

Some years ago, I compromised my health in order to do something that I thought would lead to me making a bigger difference in the world. And when I did, I had a significant learning experience involving a fair degree of pain (I collapsed with exhaustion and it took me eight weeks to recover). That's when I learnt that if I didn't get the order of my values right, I was going to suffer big time. I realised that health had to be more important to me than making a difference so I started to set some tighter boundaries around my travel away from home.

Some years later my colleague Dr David Lake and I were invited to present some 'very important programs' in the USA and Canada. But doing them all meant I would be going away from my family for 25 days. Now, I'd been doing very well for two or three years going away for around two weeks at a time and being home the majority of the time. I thought it would be fine, but when it got closer and closer to the date of departure, I suddenly got sick 'out of the blue'.

When I explored this with my friend David Lake (some things are easier to see through the assistance of others) I realised the reason why I had become sick was because I was about to compromise my number one value (love) in favour of my number three and four values (making a difference and achieving). As I now teach others: You will never be happy as long as you allow lower values to rule over higher values.

Fortunately this time I got sick—but not too sick. This time I received the warning before I had to let it go so far that I collapsed completely as in my earlier experience. So I immediately cancelled and rescheduled these events. That was very tough for me because I had made commitments and by withdrawing I knew I was going to upset many people. But I also realised if I did bad by my wife and family who were the *most important* to me, then I wouldn't be much good for anybody. So in the end I had to make the decision I made and it was one of the best things I ever did.

In order to be happy now, you need to choose based on your values.

If, like I did, you let things get out of balance for too long there will come a time when it's an either-or decision which must be resolved in terms of your highest value, but when you return to a balance that is right for you then most of the time it all works together. When it all works together you're in the right state. When it all works together you get what you want from all paths (and all parts of you are happy).

I am so fortunate that I get to have a wonderful, loving relationship and family life and also have the privilege to make a difference in the world. But never at the expense of each other.

CHAPTER 4

Releasing Emotional Attachments Using Simple Energy Techniques (SET)

When it comes to techniques to break through limits, there are many available which can all work to varying degrees. Mental, or cognitive strategies like taking control of your self-talk, taking control of your internal focus, using techniques like visualisation: they all work well for many people. In this book, I'm going to give you another alternative. I'll show you how you can use Simple Energy Techniques (SET), which can also be combined with proven techniques like these to make a more powerful combination for success.

Manage Your Emotional State

When you're feeling good inside yourself, everything outside seems clearer and easier. If you're not getting clarity it's because you've not got that feeling within yourself that allows you to think clearly.

If you approach your goal with fear, or even worse with the

feeling and belief that you can't have it, in that state how well are you going to perform? Not very well.

You start at a disadvantage when you are feeling negative and try to achieve your goal, because you start with the belief you can't have it, then you try and find clarity with that dictating the terms.

So changing your emotional state becomes paramount in getting what you want. Lots of people try to change this by changing their thinking, but this can be counterproductive if it doesn't result in a corresponding emotional shift.

The usual ways of dealing with our negative emotional states are to ignore them, to try to distract ourselves from them, or to ingest a substance to alter our state. This is what most people do: they medicate their negative feelings with food or drugs. But all that does is numb the feelings, and they tend to return later.

A lot of psychological techniques involve focusing on or even attacking the negative state. Alternatively, you just try very hard to focus on something else. You look on the bright side; you try to force yourself to go to the other side. These are the typical ways people deal with negative emotional states and 'negative thinking'.

The challenge with those approaches is the negative is still there. New research in neuroscience now shows that when you try not to think negative thoughts, you end up thinking them more. The same happens with negative feelings: *what you resist persists!*

I don't believe that real power can come from ignoring or denying the negative. Real power is being able to face the situation and that thing that used to upset you or stop you and find that it hasn't got any power over you at all. For example, you are able to think the negative thought and it doesn't upset you, or cause you to react at all. It has no power to control you. Is this possible? Yes, it is, and I'm now going to share with you some of the most powerful techniques I've learned for helping you to do this: energy techniques.

What Are Energy Techniques?

There are many different energy techniques but the one I'm going to share with you in this book is the approach I developed with my colleague Dr David Lake called Simple Energy Techniques (SET). SET is a simple (as the name implies) process of stimulating energy points on the body which correspond to the meridian points used in acupuncture and acupressure by gently tapping or rubbing them with your fingers.

SET evolved from earlier techniques Thought Field Therapy, developed by Roger Callahan, and Emotional Freedom Techniques, developed by Gary Craig; however, although SET uses the same acupressure points as these approaches, it also has several elements which make it different to those two approaches. In essence, SET is easier to use for self-help, and just as effective!

Background — How Energy Techniques Were Developed

Roger Callahan, a clinical psychologist in California, discovered the power of these types of techniques some 30 or so years ago. Following the dramatic response of a phobic client to tapping on an acupressure point under the eye, he developed a treatment system he called Thought Field Therapy (TFT), using some 12 energy meridian points on the face and hands. By integrating

29

knowledge from kinesiology, Traditional Chinese Medicine (TCM) and psychology, Callahan developed a diagnostic procedure for determining high-probability tapping sequences, or algorithms for typical emotional problems.

Gary Craig, who studied with Callahan, developed a much-simplified system using an 'all-purpose recipe', which he later simplified to some seven tapping points which did not require any other diagnostic consideration to use. As well, he developed a subset of practical coaching techniques which enable the points to be used very effectively with treating trauma and emotional disturbance. It is this system, called Emotional Freedom Techniques (EFT), which has spread most widely because of this simplicity, practicality and effectiveness. Many people call it simply 'tapping' and many different approaches have evolved.

I studied with Gary Craig and used his approach for many years. Then, together with my friend and colleague Dr David Lake, we developed some refinements and simplifications to the basic procedures advanced in TFT and EFT, and named our new approach Simple Energy Techniques (SET). SET is very simple to use, gentle, natural and very effective as self-help. It can also be effectively combined with virtually any therapy or coaching approach to enhance the results.

What Energy Techniques Can Do for You

Energy techniques like EFT and SET are emotional healing techniques and you can use them to free yourself from negative emotions and pain. In this book we'll also explore how SET tapping can be used to enhance your performance and help you to achieve your goals.

There are four main effects of using SET:

- It is very relaxing. Many people experience a relaxation effect within a few minutes of first tapping on the energy points.

- It can calm and ease negative / toxic emotions, and release 'stuck' emotions.

- It can weaken the negative beliefs underlying your emotional problems.

- There is a positive generalisation effect that occurs after several significant issues have been addressed and / or after several weeks of practice of the techniques. Many of your negative problems and beliefs tend to have less influence over you and you develop a sense of optimism and positive wellbeing.

Research has shown positive results for tapping with a large number of problems including phobias, anxiety, traumatic stress, PTSD, depression, food cravings, weight loss and a range of long-term psychological symptoms. They have been found to help improve athletic performance and have also been associated with reductions in physical pain. If you are interested to find out more on the current research on tapping, you'll find a summary on our website at www.eftdownunder.com

Theory—What Is Going on When You Use These Techniques?

One theory behind the energy techniques of EFT and SET is that negative emotions are caused by a 'disruption' in the body's energy system—meaning that the source of the disturbance when you are emotionally upset is located in your body, not just held in the mind. Tapping on the energy points is presumed to remove these 'energy' blockages and restore healthy energy flow via the energy meridians. By intervening in the energy system to correct this disruption, EFT and SET can frequently provide rapid relief from many negative emotional problems and issues as well as many cases of physical pain and even some physical symptoms (though you should always consult a physician regarding physical issues).

These techniques can shift your emotional states and help you relieve pain but their ultimate use may be for something greater: to release underlying beliefs and promote generative change, where you're expanding and creating new things.

Generative change is positive change that grows, in an ever-expanding fashion. That's what I'm most interested in: using SET to help you create a better, more successful future, rather than just using it in a remedial fashion to fix your current problems (although you can use it for that as well!).

First, we'll go through the basics of SET, then I'll show you how to build on the basics, take it further to release those underlying beliefs and then access your energy and power for change.

If you are new to these techniques, you are in for a treat when you discover what they can really do for you. And if you are someone who knows these energy techniques already, you'll learn some new distinctions and ways of applying the techniques for greater results and deep changes.

How to Do SET

SET at its most basic is a simple process of tapping on certain points on your body with your fingers. The points in SET are energy points on the body which correspond to the points used in acupressure and acupuncture, although it isn't necessary for you to know anything about Chinese medicine in order to use these points to help yourself.

Although there are a number of different points, you don't have to follow a prescribed sequence when you tap on the points. Initially, it can help to learn all the points in a certain order, by tapping for example from top to bottom, although ultimately you can tap on the points in any order and still get good results.

You can gain results with SET by applying it directly to your problems, blocks and issues. Basically, direct work with SET involves tapping on the acupressure points while you focus on any issue or problem. As you'll learn, you can also gain benefits from just tapping on the points and not focusing on anything specific. We call this process Energy Toning, and we have found that if you are willing to simply tap on the SET points for a few minutes each day you can progressively alter your reactivity to emotional problems and increase your positive life energy.

Negative Thinking Is the Way to Go Here

One thing which is initially difficult for people to understand is that SET works on the negatives, and in this sense requires the opposite of positive thinking. When you tune into a negative issue you actually tune the negative feeling into your body and there may also be a negative way of thinking in your mind. These become the targets of the SET tapping process. When doing direct work it is always better to have the target in focus.

Negative thinking and negative feeling are connected; your

33

thinking starts to stink at the same time as your feelings are upset. So most problems have a particular way of thinking and feeling connected to them and the problem is, if we just try and change the thinking part that doesn't always affect the feeling part. SET tends to work to do that because it's primarily a body energy technique which works on the body's energetic / emotional reaction. There's also evidence that tapping on these points influences brain chemistry as well as brain waves, increasing the rate and flow of endorphins, the brain's happy chemicals, reducing the rate and flow of cortisol, which is associated with stress, as well as modifying the brain waves towards more theta waves, which disrupt anxiety messages.

Learning the Process and Experiencing SET

To get an experience of SET, start by identifying an issue or problem that gives you some sort of negative feeling. Rate that negative feeling from 0-10, where zero is no feeling at all and 10 is as bad as it could possibly feel. Then apply the SET process to that problem and see if you experience a change in the intensity of your negative feelings. Obviously some problems are more complex and contain many aspects, so let's just see if you can notice a small shift from this first little experiment in applying SET.

Once you get used to doing SET, I'm hoping that you will use this wonderful little process throughout your life. For now, let's just try it out. In the following pages you will find a diagram of the points used in SET and a basic description of how to use it. Before applying it you may also wish to read the transcribed segment from my workshop which follows this section, where I use SET with a group of volunteers, to help inform you in your use of the technique. You can also go online to our website where we have extensive free videos and information on using SET: www.eftdownunder.com

Tapping Points used in SET

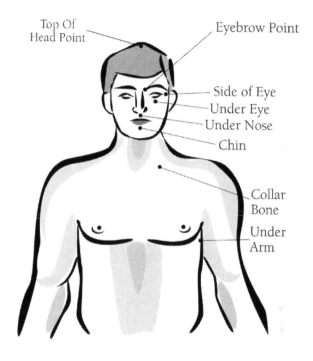

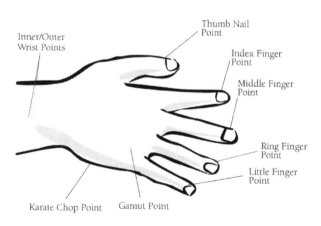

Description of the SET Process

The following is an edited version of the special report on SET which appears on our website (www.eftdownunder.com).

Focus SET on any emotional or physical problem and while focusing on the problem simply tap on any of the points shown *in any order* until you feel relief. Most people find that using two fingers of their dominant hand to tap on the points is best. Tap from 5 to 15 times on each point, or more if you prefer.

Tap hard enough to feel it but not hard enough to hurt. If you prefer you can gently rub or hold the points. Ultimately you can use whatever method you prefer to stimulate the points. The key is to get the body stimulation happening, which stimulates the flow of your life energy, and as it does so, releases the blocks. When your energy returns to flow, then you will be more able to adapt and adjust to life's challenges without being stuck in one emotional reaction.

The actual sequence you use to stimulate the points doesn't matter very much, although it does seem necessary to include at least three to four different meridian points in whatever sequence you use for best results.

Let your thoughts and feelings come while you tap. Accept every thought and feeling and allow even negative thoughts to come but add tapping to their presence.

Keep tapping continually on the points until you feel relief. Check your emotional intensity and continue tapping if there is remaining negative intensity or if other issues have come to mind. Be prepared to persist with the procedure, and realise that some problems will have many different aspects to them, and you may need to apply the tapping to each of these aspects in order to experience full relief (see below).

Even when you aren't specifically focusing in on any parts of the problem, just tap on the points continually. This appears to have the beneficial effect of 'toning' your energy system. It works even if you are not actually concentrating directly (although directly is ideal), or you don't know consciously what the problem is. Part of you does know.

Take a deep breath after a sequence of tapping, or when you notice a 'shift'.

Get some tapping into your day wherever possible without worrying about having to say or do anything specific. Most people who do this on a daily basis report that their optimism and positive energy levels increase over time and their general stress levels decrease. We now believe that sufficient meridian stimulation may cause a shift in your nervous system such that your negative problems cannot take hold in the same way.

We recommend linking continual tapping of the SET points to other habits such as watching TV, talking on the phone, or going for a walk. Make it a beneficial habit.

Don't just wait for a problem to arise to start tapping. By tapping on a more continual basis (say, 30 minutes to one hour per day) you will be increasing your positive energy and decreasing your stress levels automatically.

Consider working with someone else if you have trouble identifying parts of the problem to work on. In using SET with thousands of people we have found that the amount of meridian stimulation is a key factor in improved results and therefore we encourage people to get as much tapping as possible into their life.

In addition to tapping on the upper body and hand points with the dominant hand, you can tap on the finger points of the hand using the thumb of the same hand. This is easy to do, non-fatiguing, easy to integrate into your routine and can be done in public (under the table or behind the back if you prefer).

Any blocking beliefs or thoughts, or problems that won't shift can be treated as 'the next problem'. If you are not getting results, you can seek to identify the blocking thought or belief and apply the tapping to that. Usually you will be able to proceed at that point.

Focus on *whatever you are aware of*—mind (thoughts, beliefs, memories, worries) or body (feelings, intensity, bodily location)— while tapping.

Whilst we see the value of working specifically—focusing in on the problem aspects and working through them systematically to produce relief—we have also seen a benefit from working non-specifically, where relief comes from simply stimulating the meridian system even when you aren't focused on the problem (see below). We thus encourage you to use a lot of continual meridian stimulation as a form of 'general energy toning' and we have seen this produce disproportionate, positive results for those who do the tapping daily for 20 minutes or more.

It is just as useful to tap or rub the points: either is fine. Rubbing the points is particularly useful out in public where it is not as attention-getting as tapping.

Just add tapping to any problem routine —without trying to think too much. Apart from the beneficial effects on the energy system the tapping can act as a pattern interruption to 'bad habits' or obsessional thoughts or behaviours.

If you are focusing on the mind (thoughts) and things don't seem to be progressing, switch to the body (feelings), and vice versa.

Note:

SET is not a therapy in itself and all of the descriptions of treatment and advice in this book that refer to self-help are not meant to imply that everyone will benefit in a particular way. A lack of result or progress may mean you need professional assistance. Be willing to consult a qualified therapist or physician for more complex, long-standing, or severe issues that don't shift, and especially for undiagnosed physical issues.

Enhancing the Effectiveness of SET

Here are some important things you may need to know in order to get the best results from using SET:

1. Aspects

Some problems have many aspects to them and each aspect should be handled with a round of tapping as if it is a separate problem. When several aspects of an emotional problem are present, you may not experience complete relief until all aspects have been reduced to zero intensity.

Feelings - Aspects may be a set of *related feelings*. For example, we may feel fearful about something and at the same time be embarrassed and angry with ourselves for being afraid. Each of these different feelings may need to be treated in order to experience complete relief.

Events - Aspects may be a set of *related events*. For example, you may have had several experiences that relate to the problem you are treating, or experienced a number of traumatic events. Use the 'Run the Movie' or 'Tell the Story' technique outlined later in this book to treat these. If you have had many such events, treating a few of them very well usually means the treatment effect generalises to the others.

Thoughts or Beliefs - Aspects may be a set of *related thoughts or beliefs*. There are often underlying subconscious beliefs that block us overcoming the problem. Ask: *What do I / you think about this problem—or having this problem—or about my / your ability to get over this problem?* When you have identified any negative or limiting beliefs, simply focus on the belief while you tap on each of the points. (See below for a list of the beliefs which are typically present.)

Bodily Sensations - Aspects may be a series of *bodily sensations*. These may shift or vary in intensity as you apply SET. The process to follow here is what Gary Craig calls 'chasing the pain'. Simply continue to apply SET to whatever body sensations arise in turn until you experience relief.

A Combination - Aspects may be a combination of the above.

We recommend to our clients: Think 'around' the problem— where your *reactions and associations* take you. Be prepared to *follow whatever comes up* and **persist with the SET process**. Sometimes you may 'tap into' an emotion or situation that is more intense than the one you started with. If this occurs, continue the tapping process on this new emotion and persist until it reduces.

2. Blocking Beliefs

There are many typical blocking beliefs that can inhibit progress and prevent you from obtaining complete relief. These include identity beliefs (e.g. "I am not good enough"); beliefs about the problem (e.g. "This problem is too big"); beliefs about safety (e.g. "I will be unsafe if I get over this problem"); and beliefs about deservingness (e.g. "I don't deserve to get over this problem").

Later in the book we'll be looking in more depth at how to apply SET to treat blocking beliefs so read on ...

Here's a segment from a live 100% YES! workshop where I demonstrate how to use SET to gain relief from negative emotions with a group of volunteers:

John, Dean, Ian, James, Anne and Jane have all responded to the call for volunteers.

STEVE: So, John, what's the issue that you want to work on?

JOHN: I'm not sure how to describe it; the thing for me is planning at the moment. As soon as you say the word planning, a barrier comes up.

STEVE: Right. So, if I say planning, what feeling does that give you?

JOHN: There's just a resistance there straight away.

STEVE: So you can feel that right now? Okay, now give me a number for how strong that resistance feels to you from zero is no resistance at all to 10 is as bad as it can possibly feel.

41

JOHN: 7 or 8 at the moment, sometimes it's a 10.

STEVE: Right now is what I'm interested in; we can only deal with right now. So when you're using this tapping technique, you'll be tapping on each of these points and as you tap on the points you'll be thinking about planning, which should bring that feeling up. And if the SET works, then it will actually be having an effect on that feeling by changing the energy in your body.

DEAN: I have negative feelings when I think about going for a jog, thinking about the pain that that might cause.

STEVE: So when you're tapping on the points will you be thinking about jogging or thinking about the pain of jogging?

DEAN: I guess the pain of jogging. That's the bit that puts me off.

STEVE: If you think about jogging right now, how much of that negative feeling do you feel?

DEAN: Probably a 7 or an 8.

STEVE (to group): So he wants to go jogging and he doesn't want to go jogging, both at the same time. He wants to go jogging but he thinks jogging will be painful. Now that's either a negative belief or it's true. Actually it could be a bit of both, Dean, because maybe you've learned a way of jogging which is painful; it may not be right for you. But for now, just because you associate pain with it, you're not going to go towards it; you're going to stay away from it.

IAN: My issue is the fear of running out of money and not having enough money. It's an unjustified feeling that I've never had happen, but ...

STEVE: None of this stuff has anything to do with logic.

IAN: No, of course not.

STEVE: In fact, most of the things that control us emotionally have nothing to do with objective logic, real-world thinking. They just have to do with connections that are in our body-mind that were made perhaps many years ago. So if you think about that, what tunes you into that, what causes you to feel those feelings?

IAN: I really don't know. It's just something that I have an insecure feeling about.

STEVE: So there's a bit of that feeling there right now; give me a number for how intense it is.

IAN: 8, 8 $^{1/2}$, 9.

STEVE: Okay, so you can just call it this losing money fear, or fear of not having enough money, insecurity.

JAMES: Spending money on advertising.

STEVE: See the negative reaction when he says that? Spending money on advertising. "Let's go advertise. Let's go market." When you think or say that, it leads straight to pain for you. Give me a number for the pain, zero to 10?

JAMES: It's probably about an 8.

STEVE: It's actually more like exhaustion than a pain, isn't it?

JAMES: Yes.

STEVE: Anne?

ANNE: My fear is shaking the status quo. The work that I want to do I'm being mocked for. And I have a great fear of that, actually, really going ahead and doing it.

STEVE: Of course, because the more you go out there the more you set yourself up for people attacking you and criticising and rejecting you. How intense is that?

ANNE: It's about a 10.

STEVE: Okay, that's high enough. I know a little bit about that with the SET as well, because it's non-traditional too. So we've had to go through some of that ourselves.

JANE: I have a fear of success. When I was doing the writing about success exercise just before, this old school pattern was going through my head: "She has so much potential but she talks too much! Could do better ..." It was just drummed in, and my fear is, what if my potential is not that good?

STEVE: Okay. So what if they were wrong and they just assumed you had potential when you really didn't have it at all?

JANE: Yes, because I always proved it so and I didn't have to test it.

STEVE: Yes, and that is the basis of a lot of procrastination. Because then if you don't achieve it you can say, "Well, I just didn't do anything."

JANE: I didn't try hard enough ... Yes.

Steve: So when you think about that, how intense is the feeling?

JANE: It's about a 9.

Applying SET to the feeling:

STEVE: All right, so everybody's got their particular feeling associated with their problem—we could even say the real problem for most of you IS the feeling. What we normally do is run away from that feeling, we try to get away from it to do something else. Particularly if we're men, we say, *I had a feeling the other day and I lay down until it passed by!*

In this case, using the SET we're actually going to bring that feeling up deliberately and tune into it while we do the technique. And we don't need the intensity of the feeling to be a 10 out of 10 to work on it. You only need to tune into it a little bit. So I don't need you to really get into the horribleness of it. I just need you to think about the problem while you're tapping on the points and try and tune into a little bit of the feeling.

NOTE: In this first part of the workshop demonstration we only used the upper body points for tapping (see diagram).

STEVE: So you each focus on whatever your problem is. Now take two fingers of your dominant hand and tap at the start of one eyebrow. And while you're tapping at this point, in between your eyebrows, more towards one of them, focus on your problem and see if you can feel how that problem actually feels. So, John, you're thinking about planning, which should be enough to bring up some of the feeling.

Next, go to the side of your eye and tap on the point at the end of your eyebrow. Again, focus on your problem while you are tapping. And then go to the point under your eye at the top of your cheek and focus on your problem while you tap there. Then move to the point under your nose, in the midline, in the hollow under your nose. Try and tune into the problem while you are tapping. Then tap under your mouth, in that hollow under your mouth, in the midline. Continue to focus on your problem as you tap under your collarbone. To locate this spot, if you start at that u at the base of your throat, there is a knobbly bone on each side, which is the head of the collarbone. Pick one of those knobbly bones and just tap straight underneath that, close to the centre of your chest. And as you tap keep focusing on your problem. Then move to the point under your arm, on the side of your body, for ladies this point is about the middle of the bra band. Gents, the point is about level with the nipple on the side of the body. Just tap in there at ninety degrees and continue to focus on your problem while you're tapping. And then put your arms down, and take a deep breath.

Now most problems and most issues will have several different aspects to work through and you'll need to do this process a number of times. And there are also some extra points you can use. But for now let's just check in and see where we are at.

John, if you think about planning, does it feel the same to you or does it feel different?

JOHN: It feels a bit less.

STEVE: Okay, so it's maybe a bit less, but it seems like a lot of it is still there. There's still a barrier I can sense there, but give me a number for the feeling right now?

JOHN: 7.

STEVE: So it's taken the edge off it, but the feeling is still quite strong. And what thought do you have about planning? What's the negative thought that goes with the feeling? Is it "I hate planning" or ...?

JOHN: It comes back to getting it wrong, I think.

STEVE: Okay, so we started with "I hate planning" and there is another aspect underneath that, that you are now starting to get in touch with, which is the fear of getting it wrong. So I now want you to focus on that while you're tapping on the points. That may even be stronger than the first fear, the fear of getting it wrong and the thought I'm not good at this sort of thing, or whatever that is. Dean?

DEAN: I'm just going to go out for a jog, if that's all right! It definitely has dropped.

STEVE: Okay, so if you think about jogging right now, what feeling do you get?

DEAN: I would have dropped a point or two so a 6 $^{1/2}$ or 7.

STEVE: Okay, so do you feel less pain associated with that, maybe?

DEAN: Or maybe more motivated to go and do it.

STEVE: So that motivated feeling is coming up, which you couldn't get to before because the other feeling was in the way. It's still got some barrier there though. There is still a feeling like jogging still equals pain but it's not as strong.

STEVE: James?

JAMES: I found myself starting to yawn quite heavily when I started tapping and focusing on that advertising problem. And then it just sort of changed form and then it sort of became like a sense of lack or not enough.

STEVE: Funnily enough, when you advertise it's to get more. But what prevents you is the feeling of not having enough to be able to put into it. So the feeling of lack that's underneath the concern with the advertising and that feeling, how strong is that?

JAMES: About a 5.

STEVE: Okay, we'll continue to do some more tapping and see what happens. Anne, how is your worry about being on the outer?

ANNE: Well, it was quite interesting because I started off with this feeling but since I started tapping, fear of criticism came up, so I tapped while focusing on my fear of criticism and it has dropped it right down to about a 3 now.

STEVE: So if you think about the fact that you're on the outer and so on, what does that feel like?

ANNE: Not too bad.

STEVE: Okay, but is there still some feeling?

ANNE: Oh, yes.

STEVE: Where is that feeling in your body?

ANNE: About here (pointing to chest).

STEVE: Okay, let's focus on that part of your body there and you can still tune into that other thing but keep your attention on that feeling in there when you're doing it, okay?

STEVE: Jane?

JANE: My intensity has settled right down because I was feeling quite emotional when I first came up here. So I don't know, it's now about a 2 or something like that. And a bit of resentment crept in for a well-meaning sixth-grade teacher who said all this stuff about me which was really positive but …

STEVE: It was really positive but it actually built up this great big expectation about what you should be doing. And it is a double-edged sword sometimes when we try to encourage. The encouragement can end up being a negative. I had this thing my dad wrote when I was in grade six and it was: "Good, better, best, never let it rest, until your good is better and your better best."

I hated that note. I hated it with a passion. And it's only been recently I've started to realise that I can go with the positive side of that where previously I'd spent a lot of my life resisting doing that. I had thoughts like, "Who's he to try and tell me what to do?" and so on. And then as an adult I found I'd actually been pushing against this imaginary dad, holding myself back. What a joke! I'd actually been stopping myself from doing what I really wanted to do.

So you're (JANE) focusing on that teacher now?

JANE: Yes.

STEVE: Okay, so whatever's come up for you, now focus on that. If it's still the same feeling, you focus on the remaining feeling. If it's fear of getting it wrong, focus on that.

And let's go through the tapping points again as follows …

Tap on the eyebrow point and focus on the remaining problem.
Tap on the side of your arm.
Tap under your eye.
Then tap under your nose.
Then tap under your mouth.
Then tap under your collarbone.
Then tap under your arm.
Then put your arms down and take a deep breath.

STEVE (to John): Okay, planning; tell me what that feels like now.

JOHN: It doesn't feel wrong.

STEVE: When you came up first there was like a barrier right here (solar plexus); does that feel the same?

JOHN: No, it's definitely diminished.

STEVE: What feeling is still there? It looks to me like there is still some negative feeling.

JOHN: There is something there but it's like, because I've always known that I need to plan …

STEVE: Like you need to plan, you should plan, you have to plan.

JOHN: Yeah, a bit of it is being masked by the fact that I know I should do it, I think.

STEVE: Okay, so you've been beating yourself up about not planning. That actually makes the problem worse because we think it's going to change things, to motivate ourselves, but actually it demotivates us. It's like putting a lid on top of the problem.

Anger at yourself about the problem holds the problem in and causes it to stay. Does that make sense? So we'll do one more round of tapping and I'll get you to focus on, "I'm a bad person for not planning", because that's what it feels like, doesn't it? "I'm a bad person for not planning"; "I'm a bad business person for not planning"; or whatever your negative belief about this is.

Dean, how's your feeling?

DEAN: I'm almost ambivalent about jogging now. The motivation is gone, but the fear's not there either. I could take it or leave it.

STEVE: So how much negative feeling?

DEAN: It's minimal now, less than 5.

STEVE: Well, less than 5 still means that there is some of the problem there. Actually, you want it to be a zero. And that doesn't mean you're going to rush out and jog. But it does mean that you don't have to keep beating yourself up about it. And maybe, that isn't best for you to be doing anyway, who knows; let's see.

So is it the same feeling, just less?

DEAN: Yeah, a lot less now.

STEVE: Ian, how is yours?

IAN: A lot less, I've found my thought process has actually shifted now into thinking of what I'm actually going to do, rather than thinking of the thing that will actually stop that from happening.

STEVE: So you get to focus on your goals rather than the barriers.

IAN: Yes, which is obviously where my focus has been.

STEVE: Well, it's been impossible in a way for that not to be the case because the minute you try to think about that, this is there. And so that has to be treated in order for you to be able to focus on this sort of stuff. Give me a number for what's still there.

IAN: 2 to 3, not very much.

STEVE: But if it's 2 to 3, there is still something there; we want it to be zero.

Okay, James?

JAMES: The sense of lack has gone down now, because there is no lack at all. But a sense of "How could I be so silly?"

STEVE: That self-anger thing, similar to what John has? (James nods) So you're thinking, "I've wasted my time, I was an idiot, whatever." So you're focusing on that—being an idiot or whatever you call yourself. Keep focusing on that while you are applying the tapping in order to treat it further.

ANNE: Okay, I worked through the criticism, but then it came up with me: "Well, what if they're right and I'm wrong?" And so you know, all the stuff I'm doing, what if I actually am wrong in doing all this stuff? And I worked through that and so I'm just down to a 2 now.

STEVE: Okay, all right, so that remaining 2, what thought goes with that feeling? (To Anne) What's happened up here (upper body) by the way; I'm just curious?

ANNE: That's good; this is good here, just a little bit down here now (pointing to stomach).

STEVE: Just a tummy feeling now. Okay, you can do this in a lot of different ways. You can follow the thoughts that are upsetting you and they cause feelings in your body or you can just follow the feelings in your body, you don't even have to worry about the thoughts or words. You can just focus on that tummy feeling. You don't even have to know what's causing that feeling; just put your attention or focus on that feeling while you tap on the points.

Jane?

JANE: Probably back to the potential fear, it's probably about a 2 but there is a bit of me going, well, it's easy to be a genius when you are 10 but it's a bit different now in the big wide world.

STEVE: So now, you're like what? Little-girl-in-the-big-wide-world sort of feeling?

JANE: Yeah, maybe still not good enough.

STEVE: Okay, the sixth-grade teacher may not be the only one in there, maybe?

JANE: Oh, no, she's not the only one.

STEVE: But when you think about her, what feeling do you have?

JANE: It's fine.

STEVE: She was a pain.

JANE: She's actually a family friend now.

STEVE: You may have gone to forgiveness a little too soon. All right, well, then let's just stay on the 'It's a big wide world and it's easy'. That thought that you had. 'It's easy when you're 10 but this is bigger and more complex than that'.

So we'll do one more round just for the sake of this demonstration, although each of you might have a bit more work to do. However, as you've seen, even just doing a couple of rounds of tapping has already made a big difference.

Focus on your remaining problem and tap on the eyebrow point. And then tap on the side of your eye. Then under your eye. And under your nose. Then under your mouth. Then under your collarbone, close in to the centre. Then under your arm. And then put your arms down and take a deep breath.

STEVE (To John, testing him): Okay, you have to plan, you should plan and you're a bad boy for not doing it.

JOHN: This is true but I'm a bit over it.

STEVE (still testing): A bit over it, yeah, but not totally over it?

JOHN: Not totally but …

STEVE: We're still taking stuff we learned years ago with us right now, so when we go to do something that is similar to something that we got beat up for before, we can actually get the feeling that we're going to get the same beating. In fact, we get the beat-up feeling *before* we do it to stop us from doing it; it's a warning from our unconscious mind designed to keep us safe. It says, "You know, this is going to be bad so don't go there." And actually it is a false connection.

TREVOR (Workshop participant raises his hand and joins the discussion): Sometimes I can go down a trail like, for instance, take Ian's example, an irrational fear that the money will run out. I think I have that; I'm going to tap on that. And then, I'll tap on that and I'm thinking, yeah, I'm not bothered about that and then a part of me comes up and says if you're not bothered about that then you are not going to do any work, you're not even going to try to get any work ...

STEVE: Just follow whatever comes up. Each problem may have a whole set of aspects connected to it. Sometimes there are only one or two parts and sometimes there are 100 parts. The challenge is everybody gets to make their own connections in this world. And some of us have made similar connections to other people, and some of us have made different connections because **we ultimately all make it up as we go along.**

We go through life and life throws things at us and we make conclusions and we create beliefs. We decide what things mean and those meanings may not be correct. Our brains make decisions which are more or less conscious to us at the time: This is bad, this is good, this is the way to go, this means this, this is what that means about you and all that stuff, we construct it all the time. So in a particular area in general, you can find all of the key bits and apply the tapping to them and you do get somewhere.

TREVOR: And your experience, because you've had lots of experience now, I know you've done this with probably thousands of people. Do you find with some people that it's just a continual peeling back?

STEVE: Actually, I find that's true for all of us because we're so full of mental-emotional garbage, that there is so much stuff to work on. However, if I look at myself, I can look back and think that what I thought was freedom ten years ago is nothing compared to what I feel now. And do I feel *totally* free right now? Not really, because I've still got a bunch of stuff that I don't even know consciously that's controlling me. Until someone or something triggers it I don't know what all my issues are.

But I do know that in particular areas that I've focused on, I've been able to create huge shifts and you could do that with your problems too. Follow them. If you start on one problem, like this planning thing and then into your mind comes a memory from childhood about when you were being told off by the teacher and you think logically that this has got nothing to do with that, just go with it and focus on that because somehow that's connected to it.

And maybe it's connected in a causal way. Maybe it actually is the foundation to you developing this belief that you're not good at those sorts of things. But then you might also get something that completely seems like it's unrelated. Just go with it because for some reason those things are connected together *for you* and they are influencing each other. And each one of them that you defuse is going to reduce the intensity of the whole lot of them.

DEAN: You pre-empted exactly what I was going to say—I found my thoughts shifting and now I am not focusing on the pain of the running, I'm thinking that what stops me in the initial stage is that I work late at night and I'm tired, and I wake up in the morning and think "I'm tired" and I can't be bothered. So maybe it's getting over the tiredness that I need.

STEVE: The solution is actually to go even further back. So you work on what is making you tired but also what is driving you to have to do those things that are causing you to get tired. That's going to take you somewhere. The other thing is there are underlying beliefs associated to this. There are beliefs about jogging, and we've started to bring out some of those. And there are beliefs about the stuff that you are doing at night that's making you tired too. We'll move on to those later. So how do you feel right now?

DEAN: I've moved to tired now and on that I'm probably about a 5.

STEVE: So now you're not thinking about jogging, you're accessing the tired feeling that you have from the night before, which you come into the next morning. That's another aspect to be treated. So now tap on that feeling ... Ian?

IAN: My mind has been wondering about a whole stack of things that I haven't been doing. I've been putting them off and I'm quite eager to go and do them now.

STEVE: Interesting, isn't it? Before that, when you thought about doing them, what feeling did you have?

IAN: There's no point because if I do this it's not going to work and there won't be any money.

STEVE: Exactly, that way of thinking goes with that way of feeling. What are your thoughts now about doing those things?

IAN: That there will be (enough money).

STEVE: Yes, it's a completely different way of thinking, which you couldn't get access to because this other crap was in the way. So there is a little bit more work to do but you've started to open up something there. James?

JAMES: Yeah, probably a little bit of anger is still there over the fact that hey, you've got to put out to get back.

STEVE (humorously exaggerating): Exactly, and you've been very naughty so you need a lot of punishment! It's surprising how many of us are running on a punishment regime which we learnt when we were young and now we've internalised it and we do that stuff to ourselves. So you need to do more work on that. Where did you learn that you deserve to be punished?

JAMES: At home, and at school.

STEVE: So ultimately we may need to go back to those events to treat the whole thing. How are you, Anne?

ANNE: Oh, wow, suddenly I've got to the place where it is too hard. I'm not going for it because this is too hard to do. And so I'm still around 2 or 3.

STEVE: When you say it's too hard, what do you mean?

ANNE: Well, to organise the research and now I'm sort of thinking, well, I'm free of the criticism and the work that I actually now have to do to actually do what I think I need to do, is staring me in the face.

STEVE: So here is the thing: when you start on any particular issue, you do the tapping on the criticism. Then she thinks, Wow, I'm free from the criticism now, but she still can't get herself to do it because there is another barrier underneath that, which needs to be treated. And my experience with tapping is that a lot of people only treat one part and they don't treat the other parts. So you keep on going through those barriers and treat those as well. So now, Anne, you would use it on the 'It's too hard' feeling, which is a bit of an exhausting feeling. What about the feelings in the stomach, what's happened with that?

ANNE: It's okay.

STEVE: Where's the feeling of 'it's too hard'?

ANNE: I tapped that out.

STEVE: Oh, okay, so you got to the feeling that it's too hard and now you don't feel that so much, that's good. Still a 2 though. It would be nice to be able to have it be a zero.

ANNE: Yeah, but the feeling both in the chest and in the solar plexus is a lot lighter.

STEVE: Jane?

JANE: The original feeling is not so much there, I think it's gone, I feel a mixture of things, sort of excited about the future and also still a bit of beating myself up about procrastinating that I need to work on.

STEVE: Okay, so we've only done three rounds and everybody has shifted something. And some of you have got a fair bit more to do and others have not very much more to do; it just depends on how many aspects are connected to your particular problem.

End of SET workshop demonstration session.

So that's the basic tapping process used in SET. You can just use this same process on anything that represents a problem for you. You can use it on a phobia or a fear or a traumatic event, or a frustration or anger or anyone who upsets you or annoys you, or whatever. You can use it to deal with that feeling and shift the feelings so that the thing that used to make you feel scared or angry or upset now makes you feel fine. And that's one way of using the techniques. As we move through this book, I'm going to show you how you can go even further, to using the techniques to let go of old beliefs and inner value conflicts, and also how to use the process to help you achieve your goals and expand your life.

So stop now and give the SET process a go for yourself!

Identify a problem, notice how you know that it's a problem in your thoughts or feelings, start tapping on that and follow where it leads. Come back to the book once you've done this.

Using Tapping for Self-Help

I think it's fantastic to use these techniques for first aid, for self-help. You can use it in a situation where your fear or problem feeling comes up for first aid. Obviously in some situations out in public you're not necessarily going to run around the place tapping on those points but you can use it before you go into the situation so that you don't have the problem come up or come up so strongly.

When we first learned this my friend David Lake and I had gone over to San Francisco to train in EFT with Gary Craig. At that time David had a severe public speaking phobia, which Gary treated on stage. The entire process took about 38 minutes and for the past 18 years since then David has taught and presented on stages all over the world without any fear at all.

After the workshop we travelled into San Francisco on the bus and there was a woman behind me who had this really intense perfume on. Back then I had a real allergy to perfume, and by the time we arrived in San Francisco, I had a massive, throbbing headache. So we found a little café and sat down and I started tapping on the points. David was tapping along with me as I tapped. And we were also using another technique called Tapas acupressure technique where you hold a particular pose while you focus on different aspects of the problem and its solution. So I was alternatively doing this and tapping as well.

A beggar came along and went up to the people next to us to beg for food. And then he took one look at us and gave us a wide berth! So you can do the technique in public but it has a consequence and other people see it.

SET Fingerpoint Tapping

Rather than just using the upper body points, there are some other points located on the hand which you can use (see diagram page

35). Now THIS is something you can do in public without anyone noticing it.

Location of hand points:

The first point is on the side of the thumb, level with the base of the nail.

Then the index finger point which is on the side of the nail, on the thumb side.

And then the middle finger on the side of the nail, on the thumb side.

Next, the ring finger, again level with the nail on the thumb side.

Then there is the little finger point, level with the nail on the thumb side.

And finally, on the bottom of the hand, in that meaty area, it's called the karate chop point.

My friend David Lake worked out a process where you tap on the finger points using the thumb of the same hand to tap on the fingers of the same hand. So you can tap on the index finger, middle finger, ring finger and little finger using the thumb of that same hand. And if you want, you can also tap on the thumb finger by wrapping the index finger or middle finger around.

Now the good thing about the finger points is that you can tap on those without having to be seen necessarily; for example, under the table or behind your back. You can do this quite unobtrusively anywhere that you want. It tends to be a bit more of a subtle use of the technique. But in essence, if you tap on enough points, which usually means even just three or four of them, our current understanding is that the points are all connected and it doesn't really matter so much where you tap, it's perhaps more important that you just do enough of it.

Let's say you go into a problem situation for you. Obviously most people are not going to tap on their face and upper body in a public situation, but you can just tap on these finger points quite unobtrusively and that can have a relaxation effect. The other thing that you can do is just touch or rub or hold the points instead of tapping on them.

Also, when you have been doing the tapping for a while you can often identify one or two points that have particularly strong effects for you. Instead of doing a full sequence where you tap on all the points, you can often get quite a good effect just tapping or rubbing that point. So for me, the side of eye point works really well. It isn't uncommon to see people naturally rubbing these points unconsciously when they are stressed.

ARTHUR: Is there any additional or different value in using the six points on the hands versus the seven points on the upper body?

STEVE: I think you'll find that some points will work better for you than others. I do think we are drawn towards using certain points for ourselves, like my friend Dr. David Lake who uses the finger points extensively. I don't use them as much as he does, at least when I'm tapping for myself. I find that I get a much stronger result from tapping on the face and upper body points. Also when I tap on the hand points I sometimes prefer to tap using fingers of the other hand, it just feels like a more active approach for me to do it that way.

But sometimes I'll actually just do the one-handed tapping

approach for a long time, just while walking and thinking about issues. You don't always have to do the technique formally. You can just be stimulating the meridian points by tapping on them while going about your daily business like when taking a walk, talking on the phone, waiting in line, watching TV, whatever. Whatever works for you is the way to go. If you do it enough you'll start to feel which points tend to give you more of an effect. And it's ultimately not going to matter too much anyway which particular sequence you use. Let's say for example though that you notice a certain point is really significant for you. You could tap on all the other points and still likely get results, but it might take a little bit longer.

JIM: Thought Field Therapy places a heavy emphasis on the order.

STEVE: Yes, TFT is a technique that EFT was derived from. And their belief is that you have to tap in a specific sequence for each particular problem. It's like a key in a lock, according to the theory. However, anybody who has been willing to test this has found that there is no significant differences between different sequences of points in terms of overall results.

The key is not so much where you tap, it's actually tapping into the issue, excuse the pun. It's how you focus on your issue that becomes the main thing. To identify what it is that makes you feel that feeling, and tuning into your feeling while you are tapping on the points is more important than exactly where you tap.

The main thing if you are new to learning these techniques is to spend some time memorising the points so you don't have to focus so much on where to tap. Then you can focus more on your issue and how that makes you think or feel, and follow wherever that goes when you are tapping.

Imagining the Tapping

It is also possible to get results just by imagining the tapping. About 80% of people in our workshops have found that they can get a result just imagining that they're tapping on the points. It may seem strange to you that you can do that, but think about it. Is it easier to believe that you can use a remote control to make an appliance turn on, than to believe that you can use your own mind-body to affect the functioning of your own mind-body?

Particularly if you are out in public, just imagining that you are tapping on the points can work. I once had a lady in a workshop who overcame a spider phobia she had had her whole life without touching the points at all; just imagining she was tapping on them. After the imaginary tapping the phobia was completely gone, and has never come back.

SUE: So, in a sense, it's looking at the feeling while you're tapping and I guess having a non-resistance to that feeling being there?

STEVE: If there is a resistance to the feeling being there, it often helps to tap on the resistance first. So someone who has a severe trauma, they're not going to want to go and think about that, they have a fear of getting back into that bad feeling. So if that is you then you have to treat that fear before you can even go there. If you've got resistance, you deal with the resistance and then you can go and deal with the problem.

In the next chapter we will look at how to change your negative beliefs.

CHAPTER 5

How to Change Your Negative Beliefs Using SET Tapping

Ultimately, a lot of our lives is controlled by a whole bunch of BS! These are our *belief systems*! All of our current behaviours are basically supported by the beliefs—and belief systems, groups of related beliefs—that we've built up over our life.

Now let me give you a quick overview of how I see the world working. Much of our behaviour is largely at the effect of our emotional drives. Good old Siggy Freud said we move towards pleasure and away from pain. The challenge is, it's not real pleasure or pain, it's what we *connect* will give us pleasure or what we connect will give us pain. And what equals pain to you might equal pleasure to me. And vice versa. One person's trash is another person's treasure.

These connections between feelings and behaviours are actually the beginnings of beliefs which are also the beginnings potentially of belief systems. The belief system in this case is nothing more than very strongly connected ideas and feelings. When the connection is very strong it strongly influences, and ultimately seemingly controls your behaviour.

There are several different types of beliefs:

Specific Beliefs:

A specific belief relates to a specific element of the world. So for example the belief might be planning is bad or planning is awful or planning is yuck, whatever; that is a specific belief. That belief relates to planning but it doesn't relate to other areas of your life.

If I have a specific belief about Lisa, that's going to affect how I treat Lisa, but it's not going to affect how I treat everyone else in the room or other people I meet in the world.

Global Beliefs:

A global belief is a belief about an entire area or group. So I might have a belief about women, and that's going to affect how I treat every woman in the room and every woman I meet in the future. So a global belief can cover a whole area of your life.

Rules Beliefs:

Rules beliefs are what we have in relationships. Dr David Lake calls it the job description. He says most people don't realise what the job description is when they get into a relationship, they don't know what is important to their partner in terms of how they need to be treated to feel loved and cared for by their partner. Basically, this is your rule about how people should act and how people should treat other people. We learn this in our family, and in our culture; we learn it in our social environment, things like what consideration is or isn't, and so on. And when you meet someone from a different culture or family or social group you usually end up inadvertently stepping on their rules and you can find out that you have a conflict in rules.

Values Beliefs:

This is where it starts to get really interesting. Your values are what's most important to you. They are the *emotional states* that you want the most to experience (or avoid experiencing). I call values your *strongest emotional drivers* as they have a significant influence over all of your life decisions and therefore your behaviours.

Everything you want comes down to why you want it, what you think it is going to give you, which is the underlying value. Values at their core are your beliefs about the most important pleasurable feelings to experience and the most important painful feelings to avoid.

So this is actually very largely your decision-making central control system, it strongly influences every decision you make. The things that you think will lead to pleasure, the feelings that you think are the most important feelings to have, are the feelings that you'll do the most to get. And the feelings that you most want to avoid you'll do almost anything to avoid. At any moment you'll make the internal decision that this is either going to lead me towards one of my most important positive feelings that I really want to experience, or it's going to lead me to suffer one of the most important feelings that I don't want to suffer, and that way it controls the direction you take in life.

So values are involved in every decision you make.

Identity Beliefs:

Top of the tree in beliefs is your identity beliefs. These are your beliefs about yourself: the sort of person that you are, and also the sort of person you are not. These beliefs go with you everywhere, and potentially affect everything that you do. If you believe you are a shy person then you will tend to act shy in order to stay consistent with your self-definition. Of course, if you have the belief that you are shy, even if you act confident or sociable in certain situations you will not identify with this, and will rationalise that behaviour away.

Shakti Gawain in her book *Creative Visualisation* says the most powerful thing you can do to change the world is to change your beliefs about the nature of life, people and reality to something more positive and begin to act accordingly. Is she right? Absolutely.

How do you do it? Well, you're not going to do the Nike thing and 'Just do it' by simply deciding to believe something else, because your beliefs are not intellectual concepts. Your beliefs are locked into your mind-body and they actually have neurological correlates and energy body correlates if you accept the energy therapy theory. They're hooked emotionally into your nervous system because of significant experiences and events that have happened to you in your life involving pleasure and pain. And they are strongly associated—or internally connected—to that experience of pleasure and pain in your nervous system.

Social psychologist Robert Cialdini, in his book *Influence,* says a belief is basically like a tabletop with legs. Now there might be just one big leg, three legs, 20 legs, or even 100 legs to a particular belief tabletop.

Ultimately the belief "I am shy", for example, is just a concept. It's just an idea. And some people reading this book will have an emotional attachment to it but others won't have any attachment to it at all. So how come some people believe it and other people don't? In Cialdini's model the belief (tabletop) is held up by references (legs of the table) which support it. In terms of a self-image belief such as "I am shy" the references which support the belief are significant experiences where we learned this is true; these are the legs that support the tabletop.

In terms of beliefs that influence us most strongly, the most important experiences are our significant emotional experiences (SEEs) whereby strong emotion has become connected to the belief or concept. I prefer the term significant *learning* experiences. What qualifies something as a significant learning experience? SAPP, which is significant applications of pleasure or pain! So when you have a significant experience in your life that has strong feelings attached to it, you draw conclusions in that moment, that "This is giving me that feeling". This thing, event, person...is what causes that feeling. This is the reason for that feeling. And in that moment the connection is formed that is the basis of a belief.

It might be an experience in school for example where you went to read in front of the class and you stumbled on the words and everyone laughed at you, so you developed the belief that you are unintelligent and that public performances lead to pain and humiliation. Or it might be an experience where your mum said something to you in a moment of exasperation such as "Oh, you silly thing!" and you took this to heart. Or perhaps your dad forgot to pick you up from your tennis training and you developed the belief that you are not lovable. Each of us has a multitude of experiences like this in our past where we have drawn a conclusion when in moments of pain and that conclusion becomes the basis of a belief which can run our lives for many years until the day we decide to change things, and we can do this with tapping.

The question to ask when working on a belief problem is *how did you learn that?* Or *who taught you that?* These sorts of questions can often help us to identify the significant emotional experiences where we learnt the belief, where we learnt to connect strong feelings to certain concepts. Now the good news is, because these concepts are attached to emotion, we can actually use tapping (as in EFT and SET) to release the emotional connections and therefore release our emotional attachment to the belief.

Cialdini's approach is to challenge the references for our beliefs cognitively and to try and pick them apart, which can work. But it can be a long, slow process because the emotions for some of them are quite strong.

I see the legs of the table as having roots, so when you have strong emotional connections to that idea, it's like you're rooted to it. And strong emotions lead to stronger and deeper roots.

This is the basic process: You've had emotional experiences, you develop the connection between those emotional feelings of pain and an idea, and now the idea is held to you—and you become 'attached' to it—with those emotional connections.

In order to get free from that we have to treat these emotional attachments, and when you do that the idea can return to the universal world of ideas where it no longer affects you. So for example you can now think about planning and you don't have any bad feeling at all. Or you can think "I'm shy" and it doesn't mean anything about you at all. It has no power over you and it doesn't dictate your behaviour or your feelings.

Let's look more closely at identity beliefs and how they have so much influence in your life.

"You will never perform consistently in a manner which is inconsistent with how you define yourself." — Zig Ziglar

"The strongest force in the human personality is our need to remain consistent with how we define ourselves." - Robert Cialdini

Once we have a definition of ourselves as being a certain way, we'll do almost anything to maintain it. If you define yourself as shy and you go out into a setting where you need to do something which requires you to be sociable, then ultimately you're going to feel bad about that. It's going to take you out of your comfort zone and it's going to feel really uncomfortable.

There is a classic true story about a guy who was in therapy who believed he was a corpse. The therapist working with him was trying to convince him that he was not a corpse. And he was using a logical, cognitive, challenging approach saying things like, "Well how can you be talking to me?" And the guy responded, "Oh, this is just a figment." And the therapist kept trying all sorts of logical stuff like this without any result. Finally he came up with an idea to prove to this guy that he wasn't dead, and he said, "Tell me, do corpses bleed?" and the guy said, "No, corpses don't bleed, no way." And so the therapist pricked him with a needle and he said, "Okay, what's that then?" The guy said, "It's blood." And the therapist said, "Well, what do you think then?" And the guy responded, "I guess I was wrong, corpses do bleed!"

As this story illustrates, changing people's beliefs logically can be very difficult. With the power of tapping to affect emotional shifts, however, belief change can be made much more easy.

Demonstration of How to Change Negative Beliefs Using SET Tapping

What I want to do now is show you how to use SET tapping to treat negative beliefs and apply that to some of your own negative beliefs to create more emotional freedom. You may have a belief challenge related to how you define success. When we focus on how people define success in my workshops a lot of people bring up the issue of money and finances. You certainly will have specific beliefs about finances and a lot of those beliefs may be negative and get in the way of you being able to manifest the financial results you desire.

Sometimes a range of different beliefs and belief types may link together to hold you back, and sometimes underneath the surface belief a much deeper belief may be operating, as in the following example from one of my workshops.

STEVE: What's your belief about money and financial wealth?

IAN: Specifically that I may not have any (money). For whatever reason that I might run out of it one day.

STEVE: So it's a belief like 'I might run out'. So that's a belief about you and your relationship to money.

IAN: Yes.

STEVE: Now, underneath all of that and also operating at the same time is always your identity beliefs. Your beliefs about you and the sort of person that you are link in here. So you've got a belief about money and that affects a lot of things. And you can change that belief but if on an underlying level you still hold negative beliefs about *yourself*, then that's still going to hold you back. Let's say, if you finish this off, I might run out *because I am that sort of person.*

There are some things about how you see yourself, so, Ian, how do you describe yourself to yourself; what sort of person are you?

IAN: Fun-loving. Excited. Contrary. Rebellious. Very smart.

STEVE: Yes. Notice that some of those are positive and some of them are negative. What are the negative ways you think about yourself?

IAN: Maybe not having the necessary skills to continue on or further what I'm already doing.

STEVE: Okay. You don't have the necessary skills but if you didn't have the skills, you could just learn them, but do you have a belief that you can't learn the skills or that you're not smart enough to?

IAN: No, I think it might be an 'I'm not worthy' type of belief. Why should I have all these good things that are happening to me?

STEVE: That is a good example and it's a belief that many people have: "I'm not worthy and I don't deserve it." So you can work on all your beliefs about money but if your belief about yourself is

"I'm not worthy", then you will still have a problem, because this belief is still going to be influencing your experiences and actions. So when we do work on your specific beliefs in one area of success you might get somewhere quite significant. But if you've got this underlying identity belief still driving you the whole time, you haven't got as much freedom as you could have. This identity belief will actually be a large aspect of this success belief, and it may even be the foundation of it.

We really want to focus our actions at these 'I am' beliefs, our identity beliefs, because that's going to give us the 'biggest bang for our buck' in terms of the results in our life.

There are a lot of people who run programs to change your thinking around money—and they're very good programs—where they do a poll of the things you believe about money and then work on changing those beliefs. That is an excellent idea, but if you don't change the beliefs you have about yourself, then when you take yourself to the money you still won't be able to be okay with it, because your whole approach to money is filtered through the way that you see yourself. So this is the level that we want to work on. Let's begin …

Identity Beliefs: How Do You See Yourself?

What we need to do is to work out, first, how you see yourself. Then, we'll look at how you see yourself in relation to however you define success, or any particular subset of this such as finances, health, relationships, career and so on.

So the first question is, how do you define yourself? How would you describe yourself? What kind of person are you? How do you see yourself? And I'm interested in particular for the purposes of this exercise in any negative self-identity beliefs you may hold. The positive ones aren't holding you back so much, are they? The negative ones are. So what are the negative beliefs that you have about yourself that you'd like to change?

By the way, these are only the beliefs you are conscious of. There are some beliefs that are unconsciously driving you as well but we won't worry about those just yet.

What are some negative beliefs you have about yourself that you'd like to change?

It's important here that you identify the actual identity beliefs not just your actions or behaviours. Often when I ask people to identify a negative belief they end up describing their behaviours instead of the belief. So they say, *Oh, you know, I do these bad things.* What I'm interested in is getting below that to the 'I am' beliefs behind that pattern of behaviour. So you might say, *Well, one thing I don't like about myself is that I can't hang on to money.* Well, that's not the identity belief. That's just a belief about your behaviour or a description of something you do. The question for you to answer is, in your own belief system, *What kind of person* can't hang on to money? A spendthrift, or a wasteful person, or *what kind of person?*

TREVOR: I have what I would call impostor syndrome. Sometimes I think to myself "You're an impostor. You're only a consultant—you're not good enough."

STEVE: The book *The Impostor Phenomenon*, when it came out, was a big seller because so many people can identify with this. It seems many people in positions of high esteem where everybody thinks they are a celebrity or a champion feel like impostors. Now, they may not feel like that all the time. Sometimes they feel like they're actually meant to be there. But this is the challenge: You can have a belief that you're good and a belief that you're bad at the same time! And today you wake up and this one's winning and tomorrow you wake up and the other one's winning. That's the either / or challenge that we're talking about. Actually, that negative belief is still there unless you deal with it; it has just gone underground.

TREVOR: So it's just masked on the days that you're actually feeling positive ...

STEVE: That's right. And you build this other side and a lot of people do it but ...

TREVOR: Work on that positive affirmation.

STEVE: We work on being positive. We work on being more of what we think we *should* be. And we try to push ourselves away from being what we *shouldn't* be. But then, when *life* happens to us, it's still there.

TREVOR: Yes.

STEVE:...and really, to my mind building that positive side up is actually denying the existence of this negative side and it requires a lot of psychic energy to push it away. So what we want to do is to acknowledge that it's there (the negative belief) and treat it using the tapping, even though we know logically it isn't true. It may not be 'true' in some absolute sense but ultimately, if it's true for us, then it is true in our world, and we feel it as true even if we know intellectually that it isn't. So you know that those negative beliefs aren't true but at times you feel like they are.

So give me one of your negative beliefs?

TREVOR: I believe that I'm an impostor. It's as simple as that. I'm doing some consulting to someone and it's a multimillion-dollar business and this guy is asking me for advice and I walk out of there thinking, *I am not qualified to give you answers to this, mate,* but they think that I am and I don't and that's the important thing. I don't.

STEVE: That's the sort of thing—I am not good enough.

So this belief that "I'm an impostor" or "I'm not that good", that didn't come out of nowhere. You didn't even know what an impostor was when you were born. So presuming you weren't born knowing that, then you had to learn what that was and you learned that you are that somehow. So you've had emotional experiences where you've connected yourself to that idea.

You have to remember that really all this type of belief is, is a feeling connected to an idea. That's all it is. And because you connect a feeling to that idea, that actually sticks it to you, or attaches you to it, meaning you become *identified* with it.

JANE: What about "I am powerless"? Now when you're born, you are powerless.

STEVE: I don't think so. Not my sons. Not my daughter.

Some people develop that belief because they cry and nobody comes. Ever. And they learn that they don't have any effect on the world and they're probably quite depressed and they're not attached to people and so on. But most of us develop connections that we can have some power and control over our destiny if we behave in certain ways and so on. And that starts happening at birth.

Now, I do believe there's a genetic component. I believe that some things are actually wired in at the factory. My kids came out and they had something in them already. If you had asked me before I'd have said it's all nurture. Now I don't believe that. They come out and they have a certain amount of personality. And it may be energetically wired in, so you can pick up on your parents' energy and you can be born with some of that energy blockage already there. *The good news is that we can now influence it and we can change it.*

You can target the beliefs and use SET tapping on them. One way to do this is just by using SET tapping straight on the belief *however you perceive it*. So the simplest way to start using SET to treat the belief 'I am an impostor' is to just do the tapping while you think the thought "I'm an impostor". At that moment you're tuned into that thought and the effect of it is to some extent in your body. And as simple as it is, that process for some people will actually do a huge amount in terms of reducing their emotional attachment to the belief. However, for most of us, we need to get underneath the surface to the foundational legs or the emotional experiences which connected us to that idea in the first place.

Now for I don't know how many thousands of years people have been saying your thoughts create your reality. Do you all believe that? Not true. *It's your **emotionally connected thoughts** that create your reality.* You can have a horrible thought and that thought seems horrible on the surface, but if you think it, and it has no effect on you, you've got no emotional attachment to it, it's not going to do anything to you. It can just flow straight through. It's just an idea. It's part of the world of ideas, and it's outdated. But the ones that you have an emotional attachment to, that emotionally affect you, those are the ones that drive you and influence your choices and behaviours.

So if you have the thought "I'm powerless", and it gives you a strong feeling, then that's going to influence your behaviour and your ongoing experiencing. Twenty other people in the room might think the same 'I'm powerless' thought, and some of them will be affected by it and some of them will react like, *Hmm, no, it doesn't fit.* They have no real emotional attachment to it at all.

You developed most of your attachments from past experiences. Some of them are recent and some of them are like ancient history. They don't all have to be before age eight like Freud said, they could be as recent as yesterday, a moment ago, or last week. You can have something that happens to you as an adult which changes your whole life: a defining experience.

So here again are some important questions to ask when you have identified a negative belief:
- Where did I learn that?
- Where did I first learn that?

If you have a very strong feeling linked to the belief you can also ask:

- Where have I felt this feeling before?
- When / Where did I first have that feeling in my life?

And for either the belief or the feeling you can ask:

- When was the first time?
- When was the worst time?
- When was the last time? (that I felt or experienced this)

DEAN: I think one of the things my mum used to say, which was a positive and I'm wondering whether you know, she was of the school if you can't do something, make it up, basically fake it until you can, and you always get by. And it's a great strategy and it's worked all my life. I mean, you know my history …

STEVE: Well, she's telling you to fake it and that implies that you can't necessarily make it without faking it, doesn't it?

Dean: Yes, possibly.

STEVE: Maybe she wasn't meaning it in that way necessarily. I'm just saying every positive implies a negative. Every negative implies a positive. The way we define things in the world is really in terms of that duality, whether we like it or not. Now my dad wrote on my school paper 'Good better best' because he wanted to motivate me. It had the complete opposite reaction. Had it motivated me, it could be driving me right now to positively achieve but on the negative side I might feel like I have to keep doing it. So in a sense, even with that positive interpretation I could be a prisoner of it anyway.

Actually, *true freedom is complete freedom from concepts at all, from being attached to any concepts or from being identified with concepts, from seeing the concept as you. Real freedom is freedom from all pain / pleasure connections* and there are some people who actually achieve those states. More often people achieve this momentarily and once they've achieved it momentarily they spend the rest of their lives trying to get back there.

There's a whole lot of different ways of explaining that type of state. I've actually experienced it twice in my life. One time when I collapsed because I had exhausted myself and worn myself out physically, I had an out-of-body experience and I could see people carrying my body out and I realised that everything is working perfectly all the time, even when on the surface it appears that it isn't. I was watching myself and them and I was thinking, *Isn't that brilliant!* I could see how everybody in the group who was there was actually getting what they needed in that moment.

I've also had an experience of getting that sort of realisation using tapping, when I did some work on self-acceptance using EFT a few years ago. And that experience helped me to see that you can break through to that other level of seeing and when you do, you realise that all our beliefs about how bad we are really is just BS. And once you've seen that, it doesn't have the same meaning, it doesn't have the same power. You realise that most of the stuff that we take as the way the world is, is actually a lot of made-up stuff.

When you release your emotional attachments to negative self-identity beliefs, the feeling of freedom you get is an incredible and expansive feeling and I know this from my own experiences. You start to realise that the problems are no longer *you*. For years, I actually felt that all the problems that I had in my life *were* me, they defined me. Now, most of the time when I have problems, I think of them as problems, and *I* am not the problem. That doesn't mean that I don't occasionally still get to a place where I'm thinking, *I stuffed up, I was an idiot, that was terrible, I'm useless*, whatever. But I've never gone back to the way I was before, where the automatic default reaction was to see myself *as* the problem and blame myself. Now more and more I can focus on the problem as something that is outside of me and just deal with it the way it is. Accepting it, and working from what is there.

So, Dean, that feeling that you had when your mum did that, it was both positive and negative for you at the same time. If you do SET tapping on it and it's truly positive it won't affect it because SET **works on negatives.** So if that positive thing that she did had a negative effect and it's connecting you to this negative belief, then that part of it will release and the good and wholesome part of it will stay.

So let's say, you know, that Mum's saying, whatever it was, would you fake it?

DEAN: Yeah.

STEVE: So based on your reaction right now, I'd say that was one of your negatives. The way to treat that with SET is to use a simple approach called **Tell the Story**. You can even do this for yourself by going through the story as it happened. In that case, you're not telling it, you're actually reviewing it. Another way if you easily think more visually is to make it into a short movie. So in your case, you'd go through the movie of what happened while tapping and at any point in time when you felt any intense negative feeling, you would freeze the movie and continue tapping whilst staying tuned into that point. You then go through applying this to all parts of the memory that create negative intensity for you until you can review the whole experience and you don't have any negative emotion connected to it. My guess is if you think about that experience, there are some emotions associated with it.

DEAN: I think there are other emotions getting in the way of the things that my mother said.

STEVE: I understand. So that means that what she said is also caught up with the grief and sadness (of her death)?

DEAN: Yes. That first emotion actually wells up.

STEVE: Yeah. Of course. Which is a bit of a shame though because that means that that gets in the way of all your good memories?

DEAN: Yeah.

STEVE: That might be something which would be really good to resolve to work through. So whatever tunes you into that feeling, you can use SET on that too.

DEAN: Yeah.

ANDREW: There's probably some similar thing for me. I kept thinking that mine is a lack of self-discipline to get a job done … so I am thinking that might tie in with the root memory that my mother was always washing, ironing, cooking and putting my whites away for the week and having to cook tea each night, so she was always working. So that might be where the lack of self-discipline comes from. Everything was always done for me. What would be the connection?

STEVE: Well, first of all you can just use the connection you've made right now which is "Oh, she's doing everything for me, I don't have to do it". And then there's the other part of you that may be saying, "I don't have to do it but I *want* to do it, I should be doing it and she's showing me what I should be doing, I should be more like her." Does that make sense? Both of those are there at the same time.

Those thoughts come up any time you think any of those things. So just thinking about your mum coming over tonight will bring up those feelings and you can tap on that.

That will be one of these 'legs' (to your tabletop) but it's more likely that there have also been some earlier ones that are more significant. So what do you remember from when you were growing up?

When did you learn that you're undisciplined?

ANDREW: Um, putting into words ...

STEVE: Why am I undisciplined? Does that fit?

ANDREW: In certain areas; for example, I'm undisciplined in diet, exercise and money. Otherwise I'm very disciplined.

STEVE: I understand that it's in those specific areas. So where did you learn that you're undisciplined in regard to those things?

ANDREW: When I started putting weight on.

STEVE: Okay. So when was that?

ANDREW: Mid-thirties, I suppose.

STEVE: Okay. So there you are, mid-thirties, and you're putting weight on. And when you think about that, when you think about looking at the scales or looking at yourself in the mirror, notice whatever you're thinking.

ANDREW: And my wife telling me that I'm getting podgy.

STEVE: Ah ha. So wife telling you. Okay. So when you think about her saying that, what feeling do you get?

ANDREW: I get the feeling that I should be able to do something about it.

STEVE: Okay. So that memory in itself is part of the foundation of this point. It's connected in there. It's one of the things that proves you are undisciplined. It's one of the incidents which connects you to that idea that you are undisciplined so you can say well, of course I'm undisciplined. I've been putting weight on, I'm not exercising, my wife told me that I'm getting podgy, etc. They all support that belief.

So the way to treat that is to find one of these reference experiences / significant learning experiences, any one of them. They can be recent or they could be ancient, and just go through the story and pick up on any intense parts and use the SET on those emotions. When you do that for the entire memory and then go through the story again, you won't necessarily have the same feelings about it and when you review an event that happened to you in this way, you generally come out with a different perspective on it as well. That's typically what happens.

Demonstration of Working on a Negative Belief

LEE: I'm not worthy to be in this special league class called 'successful achievers'.

STEVE: Okay. So you're not worthy to be a high achiever?

LEE: A high achiever, right.

STEVE: All right. So here's the belief. I'm not worthy and it's actually a more specific one...You already have an emotion?

LEE: Yeah, I'm already feeling, my stomach is feeling yuck.

STEVE: Yeah. Start tapping! Where are you not worthy to be a high achiever?

LEE: In business.

STEVE: Okay. So that's a more specific area but it's still a basic feeling of unworthiness. My guess is actually the unworthiness goes further than that one area.

LEE: Yes.

STEVE: We can use it for that case, and that's fine. So where did you learn that you're not worthy, Lee, to be an achiever?

LEE: As far back as I can remember, I've got that, just that whole family feeling that we never, we're not, it's not our class. It's not our place. It's not our background.

STEVE: Okay. So this is stuff that your family used to say and live.

LEE: Live, yes. And probably things that they said too; I mean, you know, I've got family saying things like, "Oh, we're not like that" ... stories and things like that.

STEVE: Well, I had a similar thing living in Balga, the lower-class area where I spent my high school years. We used to have this inverse snobbery where we believed we were the real people and those other, richer people were snobs ...

LEE: Yeah, like we're authentic ...

STEVE: Which binds us together but also keeps us down. Australians have this in our culture. It's a very pervasive thing in our culture to keep yourself down with the crowd. And probably as convicts or settlers in a tough foreign land, it really was quite functional. But it's not so functional now.

LEE: And who am I to think that I can come from, you know, the ass-end of nowhere and do anything?

STEVE: Exactly. Who are you?

LEE: Yeah.

STEVE: Okay. Let's start getting into this a bit more specifically with the SET. So Lee knows the minute that she starts feeling something about that, she starts tapping instead of suffering, which is quite good. Most other people will just sit there and wait and just feel worse and instead of that, the minute you start feeling that feeling, you can start to shift that feeling by using the tapping. So that's why Lee has already started tapping.

LEE: Sorry.

STEVE: No, that's fine. Just explaining to the non-believers.

So there may be a bunch of other legs to this belief table, there might be some small ones and some big ones, but it really helps if we can find a specific one. Before we do that, I'm going to do step one first. Step one is you just start with tapping whilst focusing on the belief statement. So I'm going to have Lee focus on some of the statements which just came out of our discussion.

STEVE: So, Lee, tap and repeat after me, "I'm not worthy to be a high achiever."

LEE: I'm not worthy to be a high achiever ...

STEVE: I'm not that kind of person.

LEE: I'm not that kind of person.

STEVE: And I'm not that good.

LEE: And I'm not that good.

STEVE: And I'm not like that.

LEE: And I'm not like that.

STEVE: It's not my place.

LEE: It's not my place.

STEVE: Okay, let's test the results so far. Tap here again (eyebrow point) and say, "I'm not worthy to be a high achiever."

LEE: I'm not worthy to be a high achiever. You know what's coming up to me is the feeling all through my life that the things that I want to achieve meant that I was going to be different from everybody else. And that feeling of isolation is what's coming up pretty strongly for me.

STEVE: Yeah (continuing to tap). Say "High achievers are loners."

LEE: High achievers are loners.

STEVE: High achievers stand out and they're not part of the group.

LEE: And they stand up to ridicule and judgment.

STEVE: Of course. So that implies that you have some memories of when that's happened. Where high achievers were ridiculed. Do you ever remember anyone ridiculing a high achiever or putting them down?

LEE: The whole environment, being in the school I went to, that whole... even within the family, I guess, staying by themselves or ...

STEVE: Oh, okay.

LEE:...they are all...

STEVE: What's that rhyme that they used to use about teacher's pet? I can't remember. Anyway, if you did something good, did you ever have a saying like 'suck hole'?

LEE: Yeah, yeah.

STEVE: Now, just tap and say, what was the word you used to say? Those people are?

LEE: They've got stations.

STEVE: Yeah.

LEE: They've got stations on themselves.

STEVE: Okay. They've got stations on themselves. Just say that while you tap, they've got stations on themselves.

LEE: They've got stations on themselves.

STEVE: They shouldn't be trying to make themselves as if they're important.

LEE: They shouldn't be trying to make themselves important.

STEVE: People like that.

LEE: There's, you know, you're either one of those or one of us.

STEVE: Okay. You're either one of those or one of us.

LEE: You're one of those or one of us.

STEVE: And I want to be one of us.

What I'm doing with Lee is helping her to apply SET to the belief itself. And then I'm applying SET to these related supportive ideas linked to the belief, or related sub-beliefs, like "We're not like that", the stuff that she used to say at home, or her parents used to say. By doing that, we're tapping into some of those significant emotional experiences.

Now let's look at another way to do this.

Lee, can you just describe to me one sort of thing that used to happen back then, something that someone would say or something someone would do that would teach you that you shouldn't be a high achiever?

LEE: Well, I was constantly saying that I wanted to leave the town we lived in, that I wanted to travel, and I did that right from between age two and three. Um, and everyone would say, well, why do you want to do that? It's not safe out there. You know, it is safe here.

STEVE: Okay. So who's one person that would say that to you?

LEE: Mum.

STEVE: Okay. So you're saying, " I want to go travel." And your mum says that. What feeling does that give you right now when you remember that?

LEE: Right now it just feels sad.

STEVE: Okay. Start tapping and focus on the sad feeling. If you prefer to use words you can say "I feel sad ..."

LEE: I feel sad.

STEVE: And you can add the reasons why you feel sad...because going away from here means that I go away from Mum.

LEE: Going away from here means I go away from Mum. And then I also have all the fears that she had. She wanted to do all those things that I wanted to do.

STEVE: And she was held back and she couldn't do it. So her fear has been placed into you. Say, "I'm living my mum's fears …"

LEE: I'm living my mum's fears.

STEVE:…and I'm holding myself back…

LEE: And I'm holding myself back.

STEVE: "… so I can stay with her because I don't want to go away from her." Is that true?

LEE: Yeah, it is. There's a part of me that believes if I go and do this the connection that I have with my parents with fall completely away.

STEVE: Yeah. So if I move away from them and become a high achiever, I won't be able to be with them?

LEE: I won't be able to have Mum and Dad.

STEVE: Yeah. Keep tapping and say, "If I'm a high achiever I'll lose my mum and dad."

LEE: If I'm a high achiever I'll lose my mum and dad.

STEVE: If I'm a high achiever, it's like I'm making myself not one of the family.

LEE: If I'm a high achiever, I will do that with everybody. The more success that I have, the more disconnected I will become.

STEVE: So if I become successful, I'll be completely disconnected.

LEE: If I become successful, I'll be completely disconnected.

STEVE: Yeah, I'll be like a figure head with no friends.

LEE: Yeah. Like I've got to choose.

STEVE: Yeah. Say I've got to choose between high achievement...

LEE: Got to choose between high achievement.

STEVE:...and love.

LEE: And love. Yeah.

STEVE: Can't have both.

LEE: Can't have both.

STEVE: Say, "All high achievers are complete losers."

LEE: All high achievers are complete losers.

STEVE: And if I'm a high achiever, I'll be alone.

LEE: If I'm a high achiever I'll be alone.

STEVE: And in some ways you would be ostracised from your family because they're saying, "Who are you trying to make yourself out as someone better than us?" All that comes back to you?

LEE: Yes.

STEVE: Do you understand how this is actually influencing Lee right now? If you link high achievement with disconnection, why would you go there?

Tap here, Lee, (eyebrow point) and say, "I cannot be a high achiever or else I'll be disconnected."

LEE: I cannot be a high achiever or else I'll be disconnected. It sounds silly in a way but that's the way I feel.

STEVE: Yeah, okay. Take a deep breath. Okay. So tell me what the feeling is right now?

LEE: It's just that sick feeling in my stomach.

STEVE: So just put your hand on your stomach where you feel that and just tap through the points. And just say, "High achievement makes me feel sick." And notice what the feeling does and also what the thoughts are that arise when you do this.

LEE: High achievement makes me feel sick.

STEVE: And tap here (under eye).

LEE: And also there's this thought coming that, if I do achieve it, then everyone will be wanting me to not succeed.

STEVE: Of course. Because you make yourself out as someone different to them. And you're trying to make yourself better than them. Say, "I'm not better than them."

LEE: I'm not better than them.

STEVE: And it's part of you that says, I am better than them, isn't it?

LEE: And there's part of me that doesn't like that statement.

STEVE: Yeah. Okay. Say, "I want to be better than them."

LEE: I want to be better than them.

STEVE: Because they are complete losers and they want to stay stuck in X (Lee's home town).

LEE: And they want to stay stuck.

STEVE: And they can't move. Is that true too?

LEE: Yes.

STEVE: Yeah. Okay. So I want to break away from them.

LEE: I want to break away.

STEVE: It's a paradox. Because part of you wants to and part of you doesn't. Part of you wants to stay connected to your family and part of you wants to go and have another life. Okay. What's happening with the feeling?

LEE: It's settling down. The knot is still there.

STEVE: Yeah. Okay. Just say, "I'm not worthy to be a high achiever."

LEE: I'm not worthy to be a high achiever.

STEVE: How true does that feel?

LEE: Not as true.

STEVE: Doesn't feel as true. So see when we focus on some of the memories and references and associated thoughts and the things that she was told and apply tapping to them, that belief doesn't feel as strong. It loses some of the strength of the connection so the SET is working on reducing that attachment.

(End of Lee example of tapping for a negative belief)

STEVE: Who's got another belief challenge?

DEAN: I believe that I cannot get fit and healthy.

STEVE: So, there's the belief 'I cannot get fit and healthy'. Underneath that belief is a belief about you. What's the belief about you underneath that? Why can't you get fit and healthy?

DEAN: I'm fat.

STEVE: I understand.

DEAN: That's a belief too.

STEVE: Yeah, there's the objective element of that versus, you know, however we define fat or skinny.

DEAN: I believe that exercise will be painful is not the right word, but not enjoyable.

STEVE: That's a belief that we could apply SET to about exercise: 'Exercise is painful'. But I want to know *what kind of person* can't get fit and healthy? What kind of person is the kind of person that cannot get fit and healthy? In other words, I can't get fit and healthy because I am …

DEAN: Lazy.

STEVE: That will do. All right. They told you that you were lazy. All right. And to you it was like, okay, I guess I am.

DEAN: Yeah.

STEVE: Actually they think they're describing reality but at the same time describing that they're helping create it. We're all doing that all the time. As we go through life, we project onto things and then ultimately we create them. So we make conclusions about ourselves and we start to create ourselves, we make conclusions about others and we start to influence them to be like that, we are always creating our reality.

I was always astounded by this when I was at school, and for example some of the other kids admired the bikies, and so they'd start dressing like a bikie, and they'd always want to have a bike and they'd be going out doing dirt track riding on the weekends and then ultimately they'd get the bike and the leather jacket and the colours and then they'd be a bikie and then they'd say, "This is the way I am." And I'd be thinking, "No, you created it. You decided you wanted to be like that and you started attaching to that and now you say you are that—but *you* did it!"

We can't see that we're doing that. We can't see that we're actually creating those attachments. Because it's like water to the fish, we're inside the process.

DEAN: The vocabulary that I used though was not lazy it was useless.

STEVE: Ahh, all right.

DEAN: That was the vocabulary that teachers told me.

STEVE: Well, I prefer the one that they used. Because that one looks from your responses like it had a lot more power over you. Say "I'm lazy."

DEAN: I'm lazy.

STEVE: And just feel how that feels. Now say I'm useless.

DEAN: I'm useless.

STEVE: I bet you that feels different.

DEAN: It does.

STEVE: Yeah. So 'I'm useless' has a much deeper, more hurtful feeling than the 'I'm lazy' one. That's what I'm reading. Is that accurate or not?

DEAN: Yes.

STEVE: So tapping on the one that has the biggest power over you is going to be more useful.

So again, you've got legs that support that belief and you said teachers told you that you were that. Give me one example of one key time when you learned that you were useless.

DEAN: About 10th grade in high school one of my teachers told me I was useless.

STEVE: Okay, now, before you go any further, do I detect a little bit of resentment and maybe a little bit of anger, maybe a bit of irritation, maybe a little bit of hurt and maybe a little bit of something else?

DEAN (jokingly): No, of course not.

STEVE: Okay. So, before we go any further, we just start tapping, so just tap and focus on whatever feeling even thinking about that story brings up for you. Because the first feeling I got was anger and resentment about the effect that person had. What's this person's name?

DEAN: I don't remember. Feels like some sort of gorilla.

STEVE: All right. That will do. Just tap and focus on this gorilla feeling ...

DEAN: This gorilla feeling.

STEVE: The minute you start to get a feeling you start with the SET. We don't always have to get that down to zero, but there's no reason why we have to continue to suffer through the experience.

Just say, "The gorilla told me I'm useless."

DEAN: Gorilla told me I was useless.

STEVE: And even though he's an idiot, I still feel like that.

DEAN: I still feel like that.

STEVE: And I'm still listening to it.

DEAN: I'm still listening to it.

STEVE (to Dean now): Because he spoke pretty strongly. Is that true?

DEAN: Yes.

STEVE: Whether he spoke through his actions or his words, it doesn't matter. It had an effect. So tap and say, "Gorilla made me feel useless."

DEAN: Gorilla made me feel useless.

STEVE: And now I still feel that …

DEAN: And now I still feel that.

STEVE: Keep tapping. Say, "Gorilla told me I'm useless."

DEAN: Gorilla told me I'm useless.

STEVE: He wasn't the only one but he spoke loudly.

DEAN: He wasn't the only one but he spoke loudly.

STEVE: So I feel I'm useless.

DEAN: So I feel I'm useless.

STEVE: Say, "I'm useless."

DEAN: I'm useless.

STEVE: And he showed me the way.

DEAN: And he showed me the way.

STEVE: Just take a deep breath. All right. Um, what's the feeling that you have right this second?

DEAN: Still anger. Not as strong as it was.

STEVE: Yeah.

DEAN: Perhaps not as much resentment.

STEVE: Yeah. Okay. All we're doing to start off with is just taking the edge off it so we can go further. So what actually happened with this gorilla person?

DEAN: Oh, it was just because I was the smallest, shortest kid who was in the class and he made sure everyone knew it.

STEVE: Okay. So he pointed it out and highlighted it and made you the focus. And when he did that, did he actually give you the labels? Did he say, you know, 'Hey, look at him, he's useless', or …

DEAN: The language was before, during and after.

STEVE: Right. So doing the tapping on this is only going to be part of the picture. But it might be a big chunk.

Who else has memories that when they look back on them they feel really angry about those things? (Several participants raise their hands.)

One thing I learned from Dr. Larry Nims is that underneath anger there's almost always other emotions. Sometimes it's fear. Sometimes it's sadness. Most often it's hurt feelings or even deep hurt. No matter which way you slice it when someone does that to you, it hurts. You can do a lot of work on that anger and it seems like you've always got more anger, and that's because the anger is actually being driven by the hurt. So if you're ever dealing with anger, look for where the hurt feelings (or fear or sadness) are underneath or behind that and you will get a lot more productive work done.

So Dean, start tapping... and say, "It hurt when he did that..."

DEAN: It hurt when he did that.

STEVE: And it still does.

DEAN: And it still does.

STEVE: What he did was very hurtful.

DEAN: What he did was very hurtful.

STEVE: And just tap and just go in your mind, just replay him doing that and just focus on the hurt feeling caused by his actions. Just focus on the memory and focus on the hurt of that. And tap under your arm. And under your eye. And under your nose. And under your mouth. Teachers do a lot of things that end up being quite hurtful. Particularly because they're so public. And so that humiliation hurt. Say, "He didn't have to humiliate me like that."

DEAN: He didn't have to humiliate me like that.

STEVE: Is that true?

DEAN: Absolutely.

STEVE: Okay. Take a deep breath. (waits) Okay. Is it the same?

DEAN: The intensity is not as strong.

STEVE: Not as strong. So, now I'm interested to know if you think about that incident, what's the feeling?

DEAN: It's probably not so bad.

STEVE: So see what happens when you go back on the feeling, when you go back on it the first time, in that memory, you're stuck in it the same way you were when you saw it the first time. And usually when we're stuck it's because we have frozen in that moment in time. That thing has actually never been fully processed, it's still affecting us in exactly the same way. When you do this and you go through it and you do the SET, it reprocesses the experience through your body and you end up with a new perspective.

So my guess is when you're thinking of it right now, it's more of an outside perspective?

DEAN: Yes, I can see myself standing up to that and it's like I am looking back at it rather than back in it.

STEVE: Exactly. So he's now got the perspective of an outsider rather than being in it and having to suffer it again. And when we shift from things that have affected us in a bad way, we actually shift out of the participant / victim perspective or the suffering perspective into the observing perspective and we can have thoughts and feelings *about it* rather than the thoughts and feelings that we had inside the experience. That way we can learn from it.

TREVOR: Steve, what are your thoughts on the parallels here with NLP when you go back to work on a memory like this?

STEVE: I think they're absolutely parallels. I just find this is a way of actually processing the information, it's just elegant. It's easy.

TREVOR: With NLP mental gymnastics are required.

STEVE: And what they're doing often is trying to scratch the memory, if you like. Or distort the memory or reprogram it or whatever.

I'm not saying the outcomes aren't the same sometimes of NLP treatment and SET treatment. They can be. But to me what's great about tapping with SET is that you actually process the thing and you release the attachment without having to create another one.

> **Here's what I think happens when a negative belief forms:**
>
> When something happens to us in our lives that has an overwhelming negative feeling associated with it, we say "No" to it. We resist it and we react against it. Tapas Fleming, creator of Tapas Acupressure Technique (TAT) says it's a *yes* event but we say *no* to it, so it freezes in that moment, and we end up with a stuck perspective and a stuck feeling. Now every time we go back to that moment we're stuck in the same perspective and we're stuck with the same feeling. But the experience is a *yes*. And so, in order to process it, we have to accept and acknowledge that it happened and go through it to the other side.
>
> Now there are many painful ways of doing that and reprocessing it. Tapping eases you through the process so that you don't have to suffer as much as you might with many more conventional approaches. You may have to tune into it a bit, but the minute that you go into it, you usually start to move through it and I think the feeling of it moves through your system and when the feelings move through you, you reprocess the information and gain access to the learning.

I believe our feelings are meant to move us and move through us, not to get stuck.

When we have a stuck feeling we've got a stuck perspective and we're stuck in that moment in time of our development. It's as if we've never moved on. We say "No" to it as in, I can't deal with this. No, this isn't happening. No, this shouldn't be happening. But it's a "Yes". And the challenge is when you're a kid, you can't go with that. You can't work through that. You can't see the other side of that because you have the narrow view of the child's perspective. You can't see that the teacher is just being an idiot or having a bad day or whatever else might give perspective to a fully conscious adult.

KAREN: How do you know what's a "Yes"?

STEVE: It's real. It really happened. It's acknowledging that and accepting that. With some extremely traumatic events no kid who's in that situation is really going to be able to be there and bear with it and go through it. Typically they're just going to flee and people who've had severe traumas, it's like they go out of their body, they dissociate from the whole situation so they're not even there. And that's an unhealthy type of dissociation that happens, although it might be quite functional at the time. When you get over your problems, you have a healthy dissociation from the event and the feeling so that you don't have to re-experience them. By processing the event through your body-mind you are able to be informed by it and learn from it. When this happens you are able to look back on what happened from the observer's perspective rather than re-experiencing it, and you may also be able to see it from multiple perspectives, rather than just one.

So when I say it's a "Yes", it's actually accepting what's happening and accepting that it happened and allowing the feelings to move you and move through you. But they're painful feelings so we don't want to do that—we run away from the feelings. The tapping helps us to allow the feelings to move through and out, as we move from within the experience to the present moment where that experience is in the past.

In Eckhart Tolle's book *The Power of Now* he talks about an incredibly empowering perspective which is basically an acceptance of everything that is. Most people don't accept what is. They run away from it, they medicate it, they try not to think it, and so on. His approach is about embracing what's there right now and acknowledging it and then you can go with it. So what happens in this case is you normally wouldn't want to go to that memory because it was a painful one. If you go to that memory now though, Dean, is it still the same?

DEAN: No, it feels different, less intense.

STEVE: Yeah. So now it doesn't have the same feeling attached to it. Let's test the belief. Just say, "I'm useless."

DEAN: I'm useless.

STEVE: Okay. How true does that feel?

DEAN: It doesn't feel true.

STEVE: Okay. So there probably are some other ones of these, but that event that we just applied the tapping to is a significant emotional contributor to that belief. So in the moment that you release some of the emotion of that incident, you release some of the attachment to the belief.

TREVOR: How important is it always to get the specific event that caused the current problem?

STEVE: It isn't, and you can make it up actually and still get results, because you're dealing with your unconscious anyway. So even if you had no memory of what actually happened, you could create a fictitious event and tap on that because it will still have the feelings attached to it.

We might ask what sort of things *could* happen to someone which would get them to end up believing that? So if Dean couldn't remember something, I'd say, okay, what sorts of things could happen to a kid where they might develop the conclusion that they're useless? And he might say, well, maybe this kid was in class and he handed in his work and the teacher sneered at it. And that could be just as good for helping us to get access to that inner program.

TREVOR: And then you would replay that as if it was a memory?

STEVE: Yeah. Because when you replay it, you'll have some reactions to it emotionally and have some feelings come out and the tapping will help those feelings to process.

All we're looking for is a way in. The memory is just one way in. Working on the belief statement itself, that's another way in. For some people, just using the words is enough for them. One woman I worked with couldn't even say the word 'stupid', just absolutely could not even say the word. And so just doing tapping whilst having her think the words "I'm stupid" while I repeated them aloud for her led her to experience a big shift.

When Using Tapping, *Negative* Thinking Works Best!

This appears to be the opposite of what you want to do, isn't it? You want to say, "No, I'm not stupid. I'm really smart." But actually, part of you is saying, "Yes, I am stupid." You believe it and you feel it because the teacher told you it or your mum told you it. Even though intellectually you know it's not true it still *feels* true. So when you are treating this with tapping start by acknowledging that *yes* part, and the minute you can allow that to be there, it's a huge relief. It's a huge relief.

GEORGE: Some of this I'm struggling with because it feels like you're becoming a really good swimmer but you're in the midst of a tsunami. You made reference to culture before and I think we live in a culture that suppresses greatness.

STEVE: Yes.

GEORGE: So you get to the point where you're feeling good but then it's really not something that is condoned. You know, it's a faux pax. I think of (Australian boxer) Anthony Mundine when he first came on, he was so confident, and everyone bashed him and said, "Oh, what a w****r."

STEVE: Yeah.

GEORGE: And so, here's a guy that's fulfilling this, "I feel great, I'm not an impostor, I'm the real deal." The culture says no, that's not accepted.

STEVE: So you're saying, well, you can change yourself but then you've still got to deal with the outside world? Absolutely. I think the challenge is you can react against that negativity which means you try to fight the whole world, or you can develop the way you are inside yourself while realising the way the world is. And that means **you're working with the world the way it *is* rather than the way it *should* be.**

Muhammad Ali did the same thing, but he managed to change the whole world's opinion. And that's one way to do it. But most of us aren't that tough, and you don't need to be. I think that ultimately if you get solid within yourself, you don't end up having to fight against the world because you're thinking, *I'm going to create this for myself but I need to do it within this world where that's the way the world sees things.* You can then factor your changes into the world that *is* rather than having to turn back the entire tide or work against the whole world, or require the whole world to change for you.

Of course, George Bernard Shaw said that all progress depends on unreasonable men and women who won't accept the way the world currently is. Here's the full original quote: *"The reasonable man adapts himself to the world: the unreasonable one persists in trying to adapt the world to himself. Therefore all progress depends on the unreasonable man."*

For example, I can see things that SET can do and there's a bunch of people that can't even see it. Well, you can get down about that or you can say, "Okay, this is the way the world is, let's develop this and connect with people who can see it and progressively work with other people to help them to be able to see it."

Exercise: Negative Beliefs

Now, we're going to do an exercise and I know you're not an SET expert yet, but you are going to be. Because it's actually quite straightforward and without knowing much about SET other than the tapping points and the basics of how to tap, you can actually get some leverage on one of your negative beliefs.

Start by writing down three negative identity beliefs about yourself that you would like to change. Remember identity beliefs are the ones that begin with *I am*, as in *I am* this kind of (typically negative) person, whatever that is. Write down three of your own negative beliefs.

When I do this in my workshops the most common reaction is: Only three?

If you, like most people, have many more than three negative beliefs about yourself, I'd like you to write down the three worst ones.

So here's the process: We're going to do SET on those negative belief statements, starting with the first one. And the first time round you're going to apply it on the negative belief *statement*.

Below is an excerpt where I demonstrate this in a workshop where the process involves working with a partner. You can follow the same process to work on some of your own beliefs if you are reading this book. It could also be of great benefit to you and someone else to find a partner to work through this with. And if you are dealing with very difficult, complex, or painful negative beliefs it can be even more beneficial to seek out a competent therapist and work with them. Some of our problems we are just too close to and we can all benefit from the eyes of someone else. Also, some of our blocking beliefs are unconscious and a skilled other can help us to become conscious of them.

So Anne, what's your negative belief?

ANNE: I'm stupid.

STEVE: So tap on the points and say "I'm stupid", and any related beliefs you can think of such as "I don't accept myself."

ANNE: I'm stupid.

STEVE: I don't accept myself.

ANNE: I don't accept myself.

STEVE: And just tap and say, I'm stupid.

ANNE: I'm stupid.

STEVE: When you do this with someone else, you say it as if you were her saying it and then have her repeat it—the words are stated in the first person. You're leading her so she just repeats what you say. She's already told you what the belief is, and you just say the words of the belief such as in this case "I'm stupid" and tap on the first point, then repeat "I'm stupid" and tap on the next point, then again "I'm stupid" and tap on the next point, and so on. Each point we're just tapping and repeating the belief statement out loud. Then after tapping for a few minutes stop and take a deep breath.

What we're after ultimately is getting underneath the belief to, how do you know you're stupid? The beginning point however is simply to tap whilst focusing on the belief because often the underlying aspects in the form of feelings, sensations, memories and specific events will emerge as soon as you start the tapping process.

All you need to do at this point is to repeat the belief as a statement at each point as you tap.

Whatever the belief is for you. You just tap on these points and you repeat those words, so in this case, "I'm stupid." And if you want, you can get a bit more creative and add some other related concepts such as, "I'm stupid and useless." "I'm stupid and pathetic." And if some of those words or concepts or images are more meaningful or cause a stronger emotional reaction, then you stay with them.

But ultimately, you can just do the tapping while repeating "I'm stupid, I'm stupid, I'm stupid." I like to get creative with that and connect all the related ideas because I like to do more than one thing at once. But when you're first starting this, you can just start on one basic idea and you can often get a long way just doing that.

The next step is to ask the question, "Where did you learn that you are stupid?" Another good question is, "Who taught you that?" or "How do you *know* you are (stupid)?" All these things will give you some of the legs that are holding up the stupid belief.

So, where did you learn that you are stupid, Anne?

ANNE: Oh, Mum.

STEVE: Mum taught you. Okay. So Mum taught you that you were stupid.

Now when you ask these questions, what you will do is you will get a story or an incident or something that taught them that and then they're just going to tell you the story. And any part of that story that's emotionally intense, we're going to stop the story and do a lot of tapping on that part of the story.

So, Anne, how did your mum teach you that you're stupid?

ANNE: I heard her telling a neighbour that I was stupid.

STEVE: Oh, okay. Now when you remember hearing her tell the neighbour that, what feeling does that give you?

ANNE: Shame, humiliation. Betrayal.

STEVE: Right. Okay. You could just focus on the memory because the memory is connected to the feelings. But ultimately it's the feelings that we're after. So while staying in touch with that memory focus on feeling betrayed as you tap on the points.

ANNE: I felt betrayed.

STEVE: And humiliated by my mum ...

ANNE: And humiliated by my mother.

STEVE: When she said that to a neighbour ...

ANNE: When she said that to a neighbour ...

STEVE: She betrayed my trust ...

ANNE: Betrayed my trust.

STEVE: And that hurt.

ANNE: And that hurt.

STEVE: Keep tapping and say, "Mum told the neighbour I was stupid."

ANNE: Mum told the neighbour I was stupid.

STEVE: Now, in fact, I'm leading Anne but she could even just be telling me the story while we're tapping. She could just be saying okay, I want you to say what happened next.

ANNE: I felt awful. I felt ashamed. I felt let down.

STEVE: Yeah.

ANNE: I felt that I couldn't reply.

STEVE: Okay, now those are the feelings that you had. Here's a key. When you remember that right now, what do you feel?

ANNE: Umm …

STEVE: Do you still feel let down?

ANNE: I'm not sure. I feel guilty, like I shouldn't have been listening.

STEVE: Tap here (under eye), and say, "I shouldn't have been listening. I'm a naughty girl." Okay. Just tap. (Anne sighs and starts to relax.) So even that little bit, you can actually see a little bit of relaxation happening. You can often see when the person sighs or yawns. Tell me what the feeling about that memory is right now.

ANNE: Okay. I think she was just, I think she really actually felt quite proud of me but she didn't want to admit it.

STEVE: Really? So she was actually doing the opposite of what …

ANNE: Yeah.

STEVE: Wow.

ANNE: I might get a swelled head.

STEVE: Ahh. Okay.

ANNE: Might become vain.

STEVE: Wow, she was actually trying to do a positive but it had a negative effect. That perspective may have always been there but it still had the feeling about the incident.

Just say, *"I'm stupid"*.

ANNE: I'm stupid.

STEVE: Okay. What feeling does that give you now? (Anne smiles.) Looks a bit different, doesn't it? What feeling does it give you?

ANNE: I just think that's a funny thing to say.

STEVE: It is funny. It's funny. Is it true? Well?

ANNE: I'm not stupid.

STEVE: Okay. So it's possible we could find some other ways for you to feel stupid. But in this moment, that part of the thing is not so intense.

ANNE: Yeah, that wouldn't be hard but, in this particular case, I'm not.

STEVE: Yeah. Okay. So that's one of the big legs of your 'stupid' belief which has just been released.

Now, don't assume that every one of them is going to be instantaneous like this one for Anne. Some incidents are quite big and they take lots of rounds of tapping. This is just an example to get you started.

You can do this for yourself. You can ask yourself, what's one of my negative beliefs? And then, Where did I learn this? And you can go back on those memories and actually shift some of those things for yourself.

I'm just going to help you get started in treating your perfectionism problems—so start tapping. And repeat each of the following statements as you tap on each point:

"I'm about to muck this up ...
And I'll probably do this badly ...
I'm not ready for this ...
And I'm going to fail ...
I've got this performance fear ...
I'm worried about how I'll go ...
I'm not sure which problem to choose ...
I don't want to get too emotional ...

STEVE: And take a deep breath.

Okay. Those are some of the things that people have reported being worried about before when I've given them this exercise. After doing that are you now more ready to do it?

If you identify a belief that has strong emotions connected to it, just keep tapping; the tapping is the antidote. Some people get into a strong emotion and they just stop. If this happens to you, keep on doing the tapping and you should find that you keep moving through this. If that doesn't happen and you have been doing extensive tapping, then it is time to seek professional help.

Feedback After the Belief Change Session in the Workshop

STEVE: When you do this process with someone else it's incredible how many times the other person's negative belief or issue is similar to or even identical to one of your own issues. I've had so many people come to me for help who've actually helped me with my problems! It's true! And as long as you're not so far gone that you can't stay present, it's fantastic.

JOHN: And even though there was more frivolity and laughter, I think that was part of it because I saw him (partner in the exercise) shifting when we were talking about how stupid he was (jokingly), which everyone can clearly see!

DEAN: Yeah, but it wasn't stupid, you know? I didn't belong in that class. **It was almost like seeing it for the first time for what it really was.**

STEVE: It's incredible how often you can be doing SET and you can be tapping away on a belief statement that you've actually felt in yourself and even if it doesn't feel like you're doing very much in terms of the shift in feeling, you can be surprised how later on, you come back and you think, *Oh, that belief really used to mean a lot more to me but now it doesn't.* Just the process of doing the tapping on a key issue or even on the belief statement itself, without even getting into the emotions and events in other aspects behind it, can lead to a lot of shifts.

When you're working on a negative belief you don't have to get into the feeling totally. Although it is helpful to be able to tune into it, when you just think it you tune into it a little bit. It may not be enough for you to register the feeling very strongly but it's not possible for you to think about or focus on a really deeply held belief without tuning into it on some level.

So sometimes when you are doing the tapping you may be surprised to find—often later—that you achieved more than you first thought. The good thing about having the feeling, however, is that you can notice the shift in the feeling so you know that you've done something because you now feel differently about it.

When you can't access the feeling it's possible that there's part of you that blocks off from accessing it. But often, my experience is that if you do the tapping, you still get the result anyway. It's just that you don't know that you've got the result until you encounter the situation where the problem belief would normally rear its ugly head and it doesn't cause you the same sorts of problems and issues.

In this situation I would try some tapping on *fear of the fear,* or worry about getting to the feeling, and see if that allows you to access it better. It's also a very typical thing for men to have developed a system of not really getting access to their feelings. In fact we men are trained to step away from feelings and to get into concepts instead. But it doesn't matter, the feelings are driving us anyway, whether we like it or not.

DEAN (who applied the tapping to ease negative identity beliefs of being undisciplined and lazy related to jogging): I'd just like to give some feedback from me and I'm still trying to get clear in my head how it actually works and because I haven't actually got a chance to practise, I don't know if I'm going to run home and go for a jog. I just feel like I need some little key that has shown how it's going to work.

STEVE: The first thing is if you think about jogging, do you have the same feeling?

DEAN: Not to the same level but I could say that *I feel better about jogging now.*

STEVE: Okay. The main issue at the moment is that you don't want to be hooked to have to jog and you don't want to be hooked to have to not jog. You want to do it because it's a good thing to do and the right thing for you to do, and that you feel right about doing it, so that it feels like a yes to you, if that makes sense. **And it's a true yes, not a forced yes, such as** *I should be jogging.* So if when you think about jogging you still get some of those negative or no-type thoughts, there's still more work to do. If it doesn't feel 100% clear, then there's more work to do.

Until you go into the situation where the belief would normally be operating sometimes you don't fully know what the result is. When my friend Dr. David Lake and I went over to San Francisco to study with Gary Craig and he had his public speaking fear fixed using EFT, he got up on stage and was totally himself, laughing and joking just as he had the night before at dinner. He was just totally relaxed. It was fantastic. The same guy that was out to dinner was up on stage—not someone having to put on special persona—it was the same guy.

When we came back to Australia I said to David, *Let's go and do a workshop together and teach this to people,* and he said, *I don't know,* because he didn't know how he would go. His first thought was, *It was all right over there (in San Francisco) but I don't know how it will be over here.* He actually had a vague fear of the unknown so he did some tapping on the plane on the way from Sydney to Melbourne where we were holding the workshop. He was tapping for about half an hour on the plane and when the plane landed, the lady next to him put her hand on his arm and said, *It's okay. We're there now!*

When we met up in Melbourne David told me, *I don't feel bad now but when I start to talk, I know my problem will be there.* He walked into the seminar room and thought, *I don't feel bad now but when we get up there to present, then I'll feel bad.* And then he still didn't feel bad and he thought, *Well, it doesn't feel bad now but when I start talking it will be there.* And then he started talking and he turned around to me and said, *I can't believe it, I don't feel any of it.* It was just not there. And that was the defining moment when he knew that his problem was no longer.

So until you go into the situation, sometimes you don't know that it's gone, or that it's all gone. If you can think about it and you don't feel anything, there is a good chance you won't have the same feeling or problem in the situation. But you may not know for sure until you test it for real. But if you can think about it and you still feel something, you know there's definitely more work to do. Then, after you've treated every way of thinking about it and you can't get yourself upset, the thing to do is to go into the situation where it would normally come up and see what happens. And if the problem comes up in any way, shape, or form then you know what to target next in your tapping. And you keep doing so until that problem is solved.

CHAPTER 6

Values: What's MOST important to you?

Values are your beliefs about what is most important to feel or experience or most important to avoid feeling or experiencing. Values are at the core of your decision-making process. Arguably every decision that you make comes about because you choose based on your values. And by definition, some values are higher than others, as in more important. When everything is working correctly you tend to choose your higher values over your lower values. Whenever you don't do that, you tend to suffer.

Values Are Beliefs

Basically your values are a set of beliefs which control your actions. They dictate what you are more likely to choose to do naturally because it feels right to do and you're attracted towards doing it. But actually, it's a control system that's been set up earlier in your life and progressively over your life, that's right now to a large extent dictating your life. You are drawn toward certain experiences because they give you the most important feelings as far as you can see. Or probably more correctly as far as that part that set them up could see.

My friend David Lake's eldest daughter Tanya, one of her highest values is adventure. She loves going off on adventures; it's the best thing ever for her. So David's had white hair for a long time because that's not one of his highest values!

Tanya often heads off on adventure goals. She went to South Africa once, and of course she chose to go on a white-water rafting trip. They went down Level Three rapids which is actually pretty stimulating. Then there's Level Four which is really for the professionals and Level Five is for the ultra-pros. So she was out there on the white-water raft and suddenly they went over a pretty choppy area of water. The raft tipped over and she and some others fell into the water. They eventually ended up getting back into the boat, then later they went down a Level Four rapid and everybody fell out. Tanya ended up being sucked away from the group by the current and going down a Level Five on her own. Then she became wedged under water by the strong, pounding current and couldn't get out, and nearly drowned until somehow she managed to wedge herself free. What's her conclusion? Best day of her life!

Now, I'm sure for many readers an experience like that would not be something you'd call the best day of your life! If so, then adventure is probably not your highest value. If this does sound like a great experience to you then maybe adventure is one of your highest values.

Values don't just determine experiences like this; ultimately they determine destinies. Your values are driving you towards a particular way of being in the world because you see that as the way of having ongoing access to the feelings that you think are the most important feelings to have.

Values are actually emotional states of being that we're all seeking. And all a value is really is a connection in your mind-body that if I have a certain feeling, then I will have what I really want. If I have more of that feeling, that's the type of feeling which will make me most successful in my life. And the converse is if I avoid certain feelings or get to have these feelings and experiences instead then I am successful.

So the touch rugby player who wanted the motorbike, he values the feeling of power. He wants to feel like a powerful person, so he does everything in his life that he associates will make him feel powerful. He dresses powerfully, he plays a powerful sport, he wants to own and drive a powerful motorbike, he wants to hang around people who are powerful people, and that's going to make him feel powerful, he thinks. So he's driven by a need to feel powerful.

Does that not also imply that potentially he feels powerless inside otherwise he wouldn't need that so much? So the converse to the thing that we are seeking is oftentimes a feeling that we don't have it. Or that we need it and we don't have enough of it. And sometimes this is what is really driving us to seek that so eagerly: we are either running away from the opposite feeling, or we think it will be the antidote to a feeling of lack.

In my personal example, my number one value is love. When I looked at where I learned that love is important, some of that was actually driven by times in my life when I felt like I wasn't being loved, where I felt like I wasn't loved and even that I wasn't lovable. So it turns out, a lot of that was a *needy* want. I was driven by that need to get that feeling.

You didn't necessarily design your current values. You didn't sit down and say, *Okay, this is what's going to drive my life.* You're actually just running around and somehow you're drawn toward certain things and you're drawn away from other things—or as you go through life you decide (consciously or unconsciously) that certain things are important to experience or avoid, and when you live consistent with those values, you actually feel okay.

So values are the things—or the feelings behind the things—that are most important to you. And if you determine what they are, which is the first step, you can live your life and get to feel successful. In other words, if you know what you really want, if you know that you really want to feel powerful and then you can focus on accessing that powerful feeling, you get to feel a feeling that's important to you and therefore you get to be successful.

And when you do that, when you know what's important to you, when you spend most of your time on that, you spend most of your money on that, you spend most of your energy on that, you have a happy life. When you don't live consistent with your current values, you feel out of place, out of time, uncomfortable and just not right.

When you work out what is most important to you, you can then set goals that are consistent with your important values.

Get the Big Rocks in First

I love the story of the big rocks, I think it's a fantastic analogy. For those of you who don't know the story, it was relayed by Stephen

Covey in his book with Roger Merrill *First Things First*. I think it is one of the best parts of his work. Covey didn't actually come up with the story but he relates that he went to a seminar where the guy who was presenting pulls out a transparent bucket and starts filling it up with big rocks. When the rocks reach the top of the bucket he turns to the group and asks, *Is it full?* Well, some people think it's full and some people don't. Well, he proves it isn't actually full because next he pulls out some little pebbles and puts them into the bucket and shakes it until they fill up the spaces between the big rocks. Then he asks the group again, *Is it full?* And, of course they know it's not because there are still some spaces. Next he puts in some sand and shakes the bucket until the sand fills all the little spaces. Then he asks, *Now is it full?* Again, some people think it is, and some realise there is yet more space. Next he fills the bucket up with water and now after everyone agrees that it is full he asks, *What's the message?*

(By the way, in the Australian version instead of water he pours in beer. The moral of the story is, *There's always room for a beer!*)

Most people say the message is you can always do a little bit more. You can do more than you think you can. You can always fit a bit more in. And this is why so many people are stressed, exhausted and miserable, because they are always trying to do more with less and fit more into their lives when that isn't what's needed at all.

The real message is that **if you don't put the big rocks in first, you're never going to fit them in.** If you don't put the important things into your life first then your life easily gets filled up by small and insignificant things. And this process of constantly putting less important things ahead of more important things is what I believe is behind the epidemic levels of stress, anxiety and depression in the world.

So if fun, or freedom, or love is important to you, and you don't put that in first, you are never going to get it in. You are never going to find time for it.

You see this all the time, particularly with women, who tend to have the mentality that they first have to do all the work and when all the work is done, *then* they are going to relax and have fun and have time for themselves. But the work never ends.

This is also how most people approach financial matters: *I'll pay all my bills, then I will save and invest with what's left.* But then you never find the money because the bills rise up to meet the money available. Paradoxically, when you find the money first, when you take some money out up front to save and invest—what some people call paying yourself first—you still somehow manage to find enough to pay the bills. It's a strange concept because it doesn't seem right. When you invest in yourself first, you find a way to manage the rest. It's funny how it works.

The key is to work out what *your* big rocks are and make sure you put them into your life first.

At this stage in my workshop I usually put up a picture of my twins Olivia and Callum at one of their dancing concerts when they were around five years old. *I was determined not to miss any of their annual concerts, so I put the concert dates into my calendar before I put anything else in.* It was the same thing with my eldest son Josh's Tae Kwon Do gradings, our family holidays, my kids' birthdays, our wedding anniversary and my football team's home games! I put those things into the calendar first and even though I ran a busy international training and development business I managed to make the time for plenty of things like this that were really important to me in terms of my values.

So what are the biggest rocks for you, remembering that the biggest of big rocks are your values? They are, by definition, what's most important.

There's No Meaningful Goal Setting Without Values Clarification

There is no point ever engaging in a goal-setting exercise unless you are clear about what those goals are going to give you. There's no point setting a goal to, for example, get an 1100 cc motorbike and then when you get that finding that it doesn't make you feel powerful. If you know what you're really after, you can make sure your goals are going to help you to get what you really want.

In summary, values are keys to your decision-making process, they're a specific type of belief; they are the emotional states you desire the most and they're the emotional states that you most want to avoid. Both sides are there at the same time usually. The minute you want one value that implies an opposite value that you want to avoid.

For me, much as I want to make a difference in the world and much as I love recognition, guess what one of the things I want to avoid most is? Rejection. These things go with the territory. In fact, in order to be successful in this way, you have to overcome that fear of rejection or you can't get there. That's why it's really helpful to work on not just the values that you want to move towards, but also the values that you want to avoid.

Values Are Driven by Our Early Experiences

Values are basically driven by our early experiences of success or lack and we become in a way driven to achieve or avoid these feelings. We have some experiences where we think, *Oh, I want to have more of that.* Or, we feel like we are not getting enough of those experiences and then we seek them. And we have some experiences where we think, *I never want to experience this again.*

Your values, although they tend to be fairly enduring, can change at any time. The minute that my first son was born, my values significantly altered. So you can have life-changing events at any time which can shift your values. You can have a significant learning experience like I had with my health, and learn that you need to shift your values around, otherwise you're not going to be around to enjoy the other parts of success.

The Most Important Question

The big question to identify your values is: *What's most important to you?*

Your current values are the things that are most important to you right now, the things that are driving you, the things that you really want underneath the things that you think you want.

Underneath all of your goals is what you think that goal is going to give you. And ultimately what you think that goal is going to give you is the way that you are going to *feel* as a result of doing that or having that or being that.

I'm going to ask you to answer that question right here, right now and ask you to compile a list of your current values.

Sometimes it may take a bit of questioning to identify the value you really want underneath the goal or change you want in your life.

Here's an example to illustrate this from the workshop:

Dean, you want to be disciplined and out jogging. If you're doing that, what's it going to give you?

DEAN: It's going to give me more energy so when I spend time with my family, I'll have more quality time with them and also hopefully it'll give me some longevity so that I don't drop off the perch.

STEVE: So, if you have more quality time with your family, what's that give you?

DEAN: It helps me achieve one of my main goals.

STEVE: Which is?

DEAN: Spending quality time with my family.

STEVE: I understand that. But when you're spending quality time with your family, what are you getting?

DEAN: Love.

STEVE: There it is. So one of his high values which is driving these goals is actually wanting to feel that love and connection. Does that make sense?

So, if you dig deep enough underneath what you want or what you think you want, you'll find what it is that you *really* want. And if you don't do that, then you can set goals that you *think* are going to give you what you want, but they don't because you're not really clear on what it is you *really* want.

If on the other hand you know that what you want is love and connection, then you're going to be much clearer in your goals and you're going to be more drawn towards making it happen because you're clear on what's real and what's most important.

What is one of yours, KAREN?

KAREN: Um, ten acres.

STEVE: Ten acres. Okay. And if you have ten acres, what will that give you?

KAREN: Peace.

STEVE: Peace. Why will it give you peace?

KAREN: Away from all the noise.

STEVE: Ah, okay. So peace and my guess is it's not just peace, it's also peace of mind a bit too because, like having the ten acres represents something else for you?

KAREN: Uh, yes. It's about the space as well. About, um, it's about lots of things. It's about lots of things but the ten acres is the primary goal.

STEVE: Okay. So let's say you have ten acres and you have a retreat. What do you have then?

KAREN: Opportunity to give back.

STEVE: Yes.

KAREN: Um, serenity and peace.

STEVE: Okay. So these are, these are the emotional states that you're after, serenity and peace, which implies that perhaps you feel you have chaos and not serenity and not peace at the moment.

KAREN: That would be accurate.

STEVE: Of course. We're always moving away from something or moving toward something. And the challenge is, some of these things are just hooks and triggers.

So actually you want to be much more in charge of the process rather than hooked into the process because otherwise we're driven and we're not conscious creators, we're just puppets on a string, unaware of what is driving us.

Underneath what you think you want is what you really want.

Mark Victor Hanson and Robert Allen said failure to live your values is not a setback, it is a real failure. You might be achieving your goals but if those goals are not allowing you to achieve your values, then you're not really very successful. So it's a key to be able to know what's most important to you and to focus on what's most important to you and bring that into the world.

Now here's the challenge. Some of the things that you learnt were important are just emotional hooks. And you can use SET tapping to release those hooks. And that's where we're going to go in the next step. What we're doing here in the first step with defining your current values is going to set us up for that next step.

What we want to do first is to get a list of your current values and the way that we get that list is to ask this question over and over until we come up with every possible answer we can find:

What is *most* important to me?
Then, *What else* is *most* important to me?
Then, *What else* is *most* important to me?

Now when you do this and you ask what's most important, some of the things that you come up with will be goals, not values. And they will really be means to an end. But we're actually more interested in the ends that you're after, not the means that get you there.

For example, if I said to Dean what's most important to you, he might say, *quality time with my family*. But is that an emotional state? No. It's a thing that he does. It's a doing. And if you have that, what does it give you? *What it gives me is a feeling of love.* That's what we are after. So the ends are always emotional states. That's what we are feeling when we're there and when we're feeling those feelings, then we feel like we're most successful.

What's most important to you, Anne?

ANNE: Well, love. Love I think is always the top of everybody's list...

STEVE: Not everybody's.

ANNE: Well, it's top of mine. But after love comes respect.

STEVE: Respect. What gives you respect? Do you mean respect from others or respect for...

ANNE: Well, respect for myself...

STEVE: Okay.

ANNE: ...and so recognition that...

STEVE: ...Ah, okay. So for you, some long for being respected by others...

ANNE: ...you're so sneaky!

STEVE: What? What's sneaky.

ANNE: I was going to say that.

STEVE: But it is there, isn't it? It's important to have recognition. And in fact, if you're not getting some recognition, then you're not feeling like you're very successful.

You might not want it to be there, but it is there. Your current values may not be your ultimate values, but at the moment, you're driven at least partially by a need to have some recognition of what you do. And if you're not getting that, then you feel like a failure. So knowing what's driving you, that's really helpful. And knowing what's important to you is helpful too. So at the moment, Anne, you need a certain amount of recognition and if you don't get that, life is not so good.

If you were working for me, I would want to know what's important to you and if I knew that recognition was important to you, I would go out of my way to make sure I did that for you.

Without knowing that, I would just leave you to your own devices and assume that you'll let me know if there's a problem. And you would probably feel like, *there's no point working for this guy, there's no recognition. He doesn't care about me at all.* Actually, by letting you be professional and work independently as I like to work, I would be assuming that I'm giving you the right environment you need. But I would be wrong. So this is really helpful in working with other people to know what their values are so you can help them to get their important needs met from working with you— and also to avoid conflict.

So, Anne, what else is important to you?

ANNE: Well, security.

STEVE: Security. Okay. What else is most important to you?

ANNE: Health.

STEVE: Health. Yes. Okay. What else is most important to you?

ANNE: Fun.

STEVE: Fun. Yes. So if you're not having fun in your life, you are not going to be happy. What else is most important to you? Just keep asking and keep asking that until you run out, okay? Even after you feel like you've run out, keep asking. What else is most important to you?

ANNE: Oh, investigation. Investigations and research.

STEVE: So, okay. So when you're researching...

ANNE: That sort of intellectual, intellectual stimulation.

STEVE: So the state is probably more like learning or something.

ANNE: Yes.

STEVE: If you're not feeling like you're learning something new, then it's boring or there's no point in continuing. So Anne, if you were in a job working for someone else and you were just doing things because you had to do them it wouldn't be very meaningful to you, would it? (Anne shakes her head) You've got to be learning something new and you've got to be exploring and doing that new stuff. Which is probably why you're not working for someone else.

So learning may be one and maybe it's like investigating or …

ANNE: Creating.

STEVE: …creating, yes. So Anne is the kind of person who's not going to feel comfortable being stuck in a job. And if you have her in a job, then you better give her plenty of scope to go out and do stuff and put her on a project where she's going to be in charge of it and finding out something new.

Knowing someone's values means you know how to help them … and how to influence them.

Knowing someone's values, you can help them to achieve what they want, get the best out of them, and also avoid potential conflicts. And to a certain extent you can control them or strongly influence them, because you can frame things in a way that's maximally attractive to them.

Values Are Important in Organisations

When the organisation's about to change and there's a big change coming some people say "Great!" Of course, their highest value is adventure, or challenge, or learning and they say, *Oh, this is going to be real exciting.* And the person who has security as their number one value is thinking, *This is a threat. I'm going to lose out. I'm going to suffer. I'm going to be at risk.*

You will always tend to choose based on your highest values first. Just to give you an example of how important this is, one company I consulted with had a woman who was a fantastic, fantastic worker. And she had become expert at what she was doing, she was absolutely brilliant. They created a new position in an emerging area which was perfect for her. We knew she was perfect for the job, she knew she was perfect for the job, the people wanted to hire her, she applied for the job and guess what happened? She sabotaged herself. The people who were interviewing her said to me, *We did everything we could. We tried to give her the job but she couldn't take it.* But they were bound by the rules of the merit selection process. They said, *We gave her an extra hour and a half in the interview trying to put the words into her mouth and she completely botched it up.* Now why do you think that happened? I'll tell you why. You know what her number one value was? Security.

Guess what her number two value was? Challenge. So in the place where she was working, she had her security needs taken care of and there was also a lot of challenge in the job. But once she had mastered that, she had her security needs met and her challenge needs met, she needed more of a challenge. So she looked for another position offering more of a challenge. But when she applies for that other position, what happens? It threatens her number one. If there's ever a conflict in choices, you will always default back to your highest value. If you don't, you will suffer. That's just the way it is—until you change things.

By the way, does anyone see a conflict here? Two very opposite values extremely close together means there's always a dynamic tension in her needs for challenge and her needs for security. So there was always going to be a problem. But the minute that her security was threatened, she had to go back to that and therefore she sabotaged herself and she wasn't able to take the job.

Now, I did this values exercise with the staff of the centre after that experience which is why I could understand it in retrospect. Had I known it at the time, I could've sat down with her and shown her how by going into an emerging area, she was actually going to have more security rather than staying in an area which was not necessarily being progressive. By knowing what's most important to her, I could highlight the security that's going to come in a new growing area rather than the security she's going to lose from moving from her current area.

The other thing that we could do is use SET tapping to deal with that tension and settle down her inner conflict and fear of change. There's another thing too. Does having security as your number one value serve you? The answer is, it depends. In this case, it wasn't serving her. Maybe it served her very well in the early part of her life, but it wasn't serving her now. So we can use SET tapping on that belief that she needs security, as well as the experiences where she learned this, and by doing this maybe we can shift the 'pulling power' of that value for her. That's the stuff we're going to move onto now and show you how to do.

We're going to help you define some of your own values conflicts in the next chapter and show you how to use SET to iron them out. The other thing that we're going to do is take some of those values which maybe you think shouldn't be the way they are, or in the order they are, and start to shift them.

Some people look at their current values and say maybe if security wasn't so high on my list I might be able to take more risks and I might be able to achieve more. Or, maybe, health shouldn't be in such a low position. Maybe fun should be a little bit higher up the list than it has been because I've not been having much fun in my life lately. That sort of thing. But while you currently believe that you can't have fun until the work is done, you'll never be able to have fun. And that belief needs to be changed by working on the body-mind / emotional connection.

That's where we're going to go but first in order to get there we've got to start by getting a list of your current values. It is often very helpful to do this with another person and have them keep asking you the questions while you reflect on what is most important to you. They can also give you feedback when they notice you saying one thing with your words but another thing with your emotions; however, if you can't find a friend to do this with, you can also do the process quite profitably for yourself. Do it now.

Clarify Your List of Values—Then Put Them in Order (Current Values Hierarchy)

Once you have a list of the emotional states that constitute your current values, we need to put them in order of importance. The way to do this is to progressively compare each value to each of the others in the list to see which has the most potency for you.

Some people try to do this by simply looking at their list and trying to put them in order logically. I strongly advise you not to do this because this is not an intellectual process, it is an emotional process.

You need to start by comparing two values at a time in a forced choice format so you can assess which has the strongest feeling of attraction, or which of the two, if you had to do without one, you would take first, and which you would be willing to go without. Obviously in life you don't really have to go without any of these values but there can be times when you must choose one at the expense of another. For the sake of this exercise, however, it helps if you pretend that you can only have one of them, therefore you must choose the most important of the two.

Let's look at a segment from the workshop where I demonstrate this process.

Anne has listed her values as: love, recognition, security, health, fun, learning, being creative.

STEVE: What's more important, Anne? Love or recognition?

ANNE: Love.

STEVE: Love or security?

ANNE: Love.

STEVE: Love or health? Tough call.

ANNE: Health.

STEVE: Okay. Health or fun?

ANNE: Uh, health.

STEVE: Health or learning?

ANNE: Health.

STEVE: Health or being creative?

ANNE: Health.

STEVE: So health is number one. Now love already ranked ahead of recognition and security so we now just need to compare it to the remaining ones. Love or fun?

ANNE: Love.

STEVE: Love or learning?

ANNE: Love.

STEVE: Love or being creative?

ANNE: Love.

STEVE: Okay, so health is number one and love is number two. Now to work out number three we compare those that are left. Recognition or security?

ANNE: Uh, recognition.

STEVE: Recognition or fun?

ANNE: Fun.

STEVE: Ooh. Okay. Fun or learning? You can only have one. What you going to have?

ANNE: I want to say fun.

STEVE: Sorry. You'd love to just say that, wouldn't you, but I think based on what I'm seeing in your energy it's learning.

ANNE: It is.

STEVE: Okay. Learning or creating?

ANNE: Learning.

Okay, fun was ahead of the others so we just need to compare that to creating. Fun or creating?

ANNE: Creating.

STEVE: Learning then creating then fun.

ANNE: Yes.

STEVE: Okay. So we have numbers three, four, five, yes. And that's (fun) actually probably higher than it used to be in your life, would that be true? It's just that you are starting to think, hey, I want to have a bit more fun these days now that I've worked so hard. Would that be true? (Anne nods) Okay, so we have two remaining. Recognition or security; you said recognition, didn't you?

ANNE: Yes, recognition then security.

STEVE: Okay, that's six and then seven. So the full list is: 1. Health, 2. Love, 3. Learning, 4. Creating, 5. Fun, 6. Recognition, 7.

Security.

We did that fairly quickly but can you see how I did that? We just took the one on the top of the list and kept comparing it to the next one in turn until we worked out what was number one. Then we took the next one, and kept comparing it to the others until we found out what's number two. And then we progressively came up with a list of Anne's values in order. And this list only had seven key values but many people have 10 to 15 or even 20 values on their list. Then the key is to work out the order of priority of those values using this process.

Now it's your turn.

CHAPTER 7

Do Your Current Values Serve You?

What we have after the last exercise is a list of your current values, what's driving you right now. What we're going to look at next is whether your current values are your *ultimate* values, or what I call your *true* values. If you are like most people you didn't design your current values, they were hardwired into your nervous system by your past emotional experiences. Even if you've previously done exercises on values, probably all you've really done is discovered or unearthed or clarified your current values. It's one thing to clarify your values as they are currently driving you, it's quite another to get underneath those values and actually create some significant changes.

Workshop Segment: Identifying Values Conflicts

STEVE: So your current values may or may not be supporting you. Most likely they're not completely serving you. You're shaking your head, Lee.

LEE: Yes, because I know they are not.

STEVE: Why aren't they supporting you?

LEE: My top two are but my third one, my need for acceptance, is not.

STEVE: Okay. So your number one is?

LEE: Love.

STEVE: Your number two is?

LEE: Health.

STEVE: Well, yes. It may be just that some of that acceptance (value) is driven by neediness?

LEE: Yes. Yes.

STEVE: I believe underneath your current list of values are your true values. And I believe that unless you put all your values through a testing process, you'll never know whether you're just being hooked emotionally or whether this is what you're really meant to be doing.

So for me, love is my number one value and the order of that hasn't changed for many years. But when I went back and I did some tapping on my need for love and how important love is to me, and I asked myself where I learnt that love was so important to me, I realised that it was actually being driven a lot by feelings of lack and feelings of not being loved. When I used the tapping on those negative past experiences, I actually still had love as my number one value. The order didn't change. But all of the sudden I started to feel the love my family was giving me that I hadn't felt in that way before. Before this it wasn't that I didn't know that they loved me, but now I actually started to feel it and started to accept it and relax into it. Whereas before I couldn't feel that and so I was quite needy; it was like I couldn't hold onto it even when I was given it.

LEE: Are values always positive?

STEVE: No. What we've been focusing on so far in terms of values are actually the positive, moving towards values. There's always the other side which are the emotions and experiences that we're moving away from. And sometimes those negative emotions can also be caught up in the positive values we are seeking.

So if you have love on your list, it's quite likely that there are some feelings of moving away from feeling *unloved* and you definitely don't want to feel that and that's awful to feel. And maybe you've felt unloved or you fear that you will be abandoned or lost or you've experienced those sorts of things in your past and you definitely don't want to experience them again.

Lee, you have acceptance as a positive value but that positive isn't manifesting itself positively in your life, is that what you're saying?

LEE: Yes, acceptance and my need for acceptance. As in I will choose to be accepted instead of being pioneering.

STEVE: Yes.

LEE: I will choose the path of acceptance over passion which is my fourth one.

STEVE: Yes. So acceptance sort of translates, it's like 'being liked';

is that what you mean?

LEE: Yes. Being liked, being accepted, being acknowledged.

STEVE: Well, that was the very issue that you brought up before.

LEE: Exactly.

STEVE: It's like having the acceptance of your family versus going away and pioneering which is an underlying drive that you have but it's been coming up against that conflict all the time.

LEE: Yes. So actually it's played out on every level.

STEVE: Well, of course that's always the way things are. So, even some of these are things that we want to move towards, even they can be like a double-edged sword. So I had love as my number one value and there was a huge, needy part of that. I look back and now I can see that. I would tell my kids I love them all the time and tell my wife I love her all the time and then I also wanted her to tell me that she loves me all the time because part of me was feeling like maybe she doesn't. And so I was seeking that feeling of being loved and actually what I was seeking was a false security because I really needed to find the true security and love inside myself. Back then I was trying to get her to tell me I'm loved in order to feel that. But that was not true. When I used tapping to release my attachment to the unloved feelings I was able to be open to feeling and experiencing and even expressing love more freely.

JOHN: Are you saying that you can change these values in a way that suits your purpose?

STEVE: You can't fool your own system. I prefer to say you can put them through a testing process whereby if they stand up to the test, they are real. If they don't stand up to that, then they're just emotional hooks, many of which were programmed in when you were a kid and you can release that attachment, you no longer need that.

You can't change this with willpower alone so the key is in releasing the emotional attachments.

JOHN: Is it worth acknowledging the values that maybe have never been challenged?

STEVE: I actually think all of our values should be challenged, even the ones which we are most attached to. I think we should ask ourselves these questions for all of our values: *Where did I learn that this value is most important? Where did I learn that love is most important? Where did I learn that freedom is most important? Where did I learn that health is most important?*

Let's say for example you look back on this and you find out, *Oh, my gosh, I learned health was important because Grandad died and I was there and I've got all this grief associated with his death.* And then your version of actually going for health means that you've got to be worried about your health all the time, you've got to be constantly thinking about everything you put in your mouth and you're obsessed with that and you can't ever relax. And when you bring that up to the tapping challenge and you treat yourself for that need, your health value may change in terms of its level of priority—first of all, it may not need to be right at the top of the hierarchy for you to still take good care of yourself. Secondly, if it stays at the top because it truly is important to you, maybe now you can actually relax more about it. You don't have the negative part of it, the tension, the stress or the needy part of it.

So, what we need to do first is to get a list of your current values in order. And then we're going to do some work on any conflicts that exist between any of the values on your list.

So for Lee, with acceptance being so high on her values list she feels it's actually holding her back and preventing her from being able to do what she really wants to do. Is that true, Lee?

LEE: Correct.

STEVE: Yes. And what's underneath it that you believe should be higher?

LEE: Passion.

STEVE: Where's that?

LEE: I think I rated it four. But I mean, you know, if I'm going to choose acceptance over passion that means I'm always going to be held back.

STEVE: So you actually have a conflict between those two.

LEE: Yes.

STEVE: So when you look at your list, see if there are any conflicts there and also we're going to look at the items on your list and see if any of them were changed to lower or higher in the order, might you actually be able to have a better life?

Even if your order ends up staying the same, we can still work on the emotional roots of each of your values like I did with my love value and use tapping to treat any of the negative emotional experiences which taught you that value was so important.

One of the things that I realised when I treated myself using tapping for the emotional roots of my love value is I don't have to be an intergalactic megastar to get what I want. What I want most is already here. And it stopped me from having to feel like I had to do so much in order to feel okay. That doesn't mean I still don't want to make a difference in the world, it just means I can do so coming from a place of love and generosity of spirit rather than being driven to do so as a misguided way of gaining love and approval.

I think it's good to question all of your values to see how solid they are. This is a chance to ask, *Is this what I really want? Is this what I really want to be doing with my life?*

I think unless we do that every now and then, we end up getting caught up in the current and we may end up somewhere we don't want to be.

JAMES: I went through my values list last night and found it very interesting that the bottom ones I put in order of importance were in fact the ones that I already have in my life. I've sort of downplayed them. The ones that were at the top of my list are actually things that in lots of ways, I deny myself.

STEVE: Tell us how that works. What are the ones that you deny yourself and what are the ones that you get?

JAMES: The ones I deny myself, I've put honesty, clarity and certainty as sort of the one single sort of value, but they are also mixed up together.

STEVE: Honesty, clarity and certainty are all one value?

JAMES: It might sound a little funny, but that's how I'll say it.

STEVE: It sounds unclear to me.

JAMES: I just feel that I really need to be clear and honest with myself.

STEVE: It's really that concept; you couldn't come up with an exact word for it. That's what the concept covers. Fair enough. Where is that on your list?

JAMES: Top.

STEVE: That's number one. What's next?

JAMES: Security. Recognition. Abundance.

STEVE: Anybody see any challenges so far?

JAMES: Slight confusion.

STEVE: You don't have to go far to find out what people's biggest challenges are. That's caught up in values often. These types of beliefs are really crucial to every decision you make. What's next?

JAMES: Friendship.

STEVE: Friendship. Friendship is a thing or a vehicle for getting the values you want. What does it give you? If you have friendships, what do you get from those? You probably get a range of things from them.

JAMES: Perhaps a bit of security in a funny sort of way.

STEVE: Friendship gives you security. What else does it give you?

JAMES: A feeling of acceptance.

STEVE: In this case, it's more the acceptance part that you are emphasising?

JAMES: Probably.

STEVE: Acceptance. Maybe a bit of recognition comes from friendship as well. The things that people typically get from friendship are connection, love, fun, adventure, acceptance, security, support. Anything else?

JAMES: Helping others.

STEVE: A feeling like you are helping?

JAMES: Yes. Learning / curiosity.

STEVE: They might even be two separate things, but we'll put them together for now. What else?

JAMES: Love, health. Fun / passion. Respect.

STEVE: And one more will do.

JAMES: Meaning.

STEVE: You say you are getting these (the ones at the bottom of the list), but these (the ones at the top of the list) are the ones that you desire or want or feel you don't have.

JAMES: Yes.

STEVE: I would say that your current values list is actually the reverse of what you've written.

JAMES: That's what I sort of realised when I looked at what I was doing. That, perhaps, is the case.

STEVE: There's what you *say* is important and then what actually *is* important to you. This is the *is* and this is the *desire,* if you like. This is the way that we think of it that's not true. You think, *Okay, if I actually go for this, I'm going to be giving up and not getting those other things.* That's not the way it really works. Actually, they've got to all work together.

CHAPTER 8

Values conflicts: The Challenge of Either / Or Thinking

If you're thinking of values in an *either/or* way, then you will act in an *either/or* way, and you will get results in an *either/or* way. You'll miss out on things you want because in your frame, in your belief, you can't have those other things. You're stuck in that belief box.

There's a range of different exercises you can do on these values to help you get out of the bind of either-or thinking and iron out conflicts in your values. Let's look at one of them...

Workshop Example: Identifying Values Conflicts

This segment follows on from the previous chapter where Steve worked with James on his values.

STEVE: James, you've got a potential conflict between security and abundance which is a big one for you, I imagine. And then there's also a conflict for you between the top half and the bottom half of your values list. You're thinking, *I'm missing out on these things and I'm allowing myself to have these things. Why can't I have them?*

DEAN: Well, everyone knows my story about the jogging and, yes, after the tapping we did yesterday on this I went for a walk this morning! The interesting thing about my list is that I put health at the top because my mind was saying, *We need health otherwise we can't have all these other things.* But in reality, when it comes to the crunch, I'd rather have a bit of fun and a beer and stay in bed. In reality, on my real list, health is at the bottom—it should be number nine out of nine.

STEVE: Exactly. That's the truth of your behaviour. So your current values are what's *actually* driving you. It's not what you think *should* be driving you. It's what's actually happening right now. And you can judge that by your behaviour and your results. The truth is it's number nine emotionally and energetically and intellectually you want it to be higher. **It's not going to go higher just by putting it on top of the list.** Those feelings about it are, *It feels like no fun. It feels like pain. And* you've got evidence of that. So why would you do it unless it becomes more fun or at least easier to do? And then it actually gives you something. It doesn't have that pain associated with it. It's not going to shift on its own, is what I'm saying. And using willpower to change when you're working against your own energy system and strong emotional connections won't work long term.

Who has actually ended up with a list that they say are their current values but actually they are the values that they would *like* to have?

SANDRA: What I have noticed is that the list that I have written is the wish list for my values. This is probably the thing that I do believe, but when I wrote it, really I wasn't being very present to my real and current values. My life does not reflect any of these. I've got fun on my list but I'm not fun. I've got spirituality but I'm boring. I'm really clear that this list—it might be the things that I value in truth. However, they're not the things I need on a daily basis. I need to redo my list because it doesn't reflect my life at all.

BILL: I have one thought. I was looking at my list and realised, *Oh, damn! I haven't put down spirituality.* I realised that it's not on my conscious horizon. That's one of the things that need to be there.

STEVE: It's on the desire list. For the moment, it doesn't come up naturally. It doesn't come into your consciousness all the time on its own. You're not instantly attracted toward it all the time.

BILL: I guess that kind of gets back to what I was thinking yesterday. Until we're threatened with the inability to actually practise those things, that's when it becomes important. For instance, if you're not able to practise your spirituality, or if we didn't have freedom. No one is writing freedom, because we have freedom. Until that is threatened, it's not valued.

STEVE: Some people have freedom as a value and they'll do anything to protect their freedoms. They enter a room looking for the exits.

BILL: I found it quite interesting because I am the cause of all my problems, I can honestly say, that when you look at it we are the cause of all our problems. We accept the issues that we want to put on board and we don't take steps about it.

It has been quite eye-opening for me. It's leading me down the path of rethinking my values.

STEVE: I think it's good that you're questioning these things. You're saying, *I'm not sure if I like the box that I'm stuck in. I'm not sure if I want to keep being stuck in this box.* It's not just a matter of deciding and saying, *I'm going to shift this.* Because these things are hardwired into our nervous system and our energy system.

Change the Connections or Fight Yourself to Change—It's Your Choice

Let's say you have a craving for chocolate and you decide that you want to change this. When you're offered some chocolate you can say internally, *I'm not going to eat the chocolate.* But when you see the chocolate, you have an instant attraction. Now you're fighting yourself to not do it. You've got to impose something onto yourself. Give yourself pain and try to make the pain stronger than the attraction. But you haven't actually stopped that attractive force. All you've done is beat yourself up or come up with something which is more painful or more pleasurable to focus on but that internal connection hasn't changed. We need to do something to change those connections.

TREVOR: One of the things that I thought was really valuable is that I had my top four values which I have previously identified and before I had never pushed beyond them. I was sitting with Anne and she said, *What are the others?* By forcing myself to look at them, one came up which was number five, which is a value that I don't want. And it is something that is causing me problems and I need to address.

STEVE: So what is that, may I ask? You've piqued my curiosity.

TREVOR: I'm trying to get recognition. It's probably a euphemism. The moral is I need to be liked. If I'm not liked, that troubles me. But I don't want this. I cannot want that. It's the dark side.

STEVE: It (recognition) shouldn't be there, but it is.

TREVOR: Yes. I don't want that to be up there. It's nudging up there against high values that are really important to me but it's reflected in my life. I will do things to make people like me sometimes to the detriment of other values. That's almost quite hideous.

STEVE (humorously exaggerating): It is. It's disgusting!

I know a little bit about that myself. I did a session with Frank Farrelly some years back, and I was talking about the struggles I was having with achieving my goals. He described this great image of all these big crowds and they are all cheering, and here is Steve with his need for recognition. As he describes it I'm thinking, *Yuck!* That's what you are almost doing right now. And Frank pronounced: *Super Steve needs recognition!* He was really drumming it into me. It really kind of hit me that *Yeah, I do.*

And the minute that you acknowledge that there is firstly a validation of the internal truth that's been running you, the part of you that says, *I don't want that to be true, but it is.* So you have to acknowledge that that's true and you also have to acknowledge that if you are not getting that, then you're not feeling so good. Therefore, you can cut yourself a little slack and allow yourself to be someone who wants recognition. And as soon as you acknowledge where you are and accept where you are that is the only place where you can start to change how you are, so bringing that previously unconscious need to the surface and making it conscious is the starting point for that. Then you can start to look at where you learned that recognition was so important, and use tapping to release some of those hooks.

JESS: Another one, Steve, we talked about last night. I'd always had connectiveness or that desire or whatever it is that I get from being connected with people. I went to sleep last night saying, *It's not right. It's not the word.* This morning, belonging came up. That fits and just sits so much better as my number one.

STEVE: So now the big question to ask yourself is, *Why is that number one? How did that get to be number one? When and where did you learn that was important?*

Usually, you learnt that it was important either because of experiences that you had where you got an injection of that or experiences where you didn't have it and you didn't feel that you belonged. That was a bad thing. You wanted to belong so you made that super important.

If you can treat yourself for that need, then belonging might still be there as one of your values, but the burden part of that or the painful, sad, or hurtful emotions from the past won't be driving it. You just have to start by asking the question: *Where did I learn that this is important?*

We'll actually address these values with tapping like we did with the beliefs. Values after all are nothing more than beliefs about what's important to feel.

ANNE: I had a similar thing. I wrote down desire to be part of the group which I guess is belonging. And Dean suggested is that fraternity, and I said no, it's actually protection which I think is really positive. I've realised that's on the list right up against being original and individuality—so it's a straight-up kind of conflict.

STEVE: Of course if you've got to be original and creative, you're going to have risk, criticism and rejection and all those things that you don't want. If we were to extend this exercise and start looking at your *away from* values, the ones that you want to avoid, rejection and public humiliation is probably high on your list. You would do a lot to avoid that pain. And that avoidance stops you from being able to get to *the pleasure that you want* most.

Identify Your Values Conflicts

If you are like most people you should be able to identify some conflicts within your current list of values. Perhaps you have a value or two on your list where you would like to settle down the intensity of that need and you would like to not need that so much? Or perhaps you have a value where if you didn't need that so much, you'd have more of what you want, or another value might be able to move higher up?

An example of this is a woman I worked with in a workshop in the USA some years back. She had passion as her number one value, which meant for her passionately fighting for what she believes in, but the problem was that she was ending up fighting everyone and it was wearing her out! And lower down her list, at number four, was contribution. She really wanted to contribute more but all her energy was being taken up fighting passionately! When I asked her where she learned that passion was so

163

important, she told me how when she was younger her father used to physically try to push her and lock her in the closet and force her to fight her way out. I think he was trying to teach her to stick up for herself in a strange way, but her elder brother used to do it too, just for fun. So now whenever she thought that someone might be trying to hem her in or box her in, in some way, she finds herself having to fight. And she was doing it all the time; in fact, many people in the workshop found her to be a bit of a pain! So here is a classic example of one value which is high on the list which could come down and one that is lower on the list that could rise up if it did so. These values weren't really opposites but the energy being used up by one of them was preventing the other from being able to be fully expressed in the best possible way.

Ask yourself first if there is an obvious conflict in any of your values, like James had, between two apparent opposite values, between his security need and abundance desires. That's like a polarity. Those are quite close to each other on his list and they are apparent opposites. It's like the poles of two magnets and they are having a repulsive effect or repellent effect on each other rather than working together.

Let's Look at Some More Workshop Values Conflict Examples:

ETHAN: Having fun and health.

STEVE: Yes.

ETHAN: The jogging thing. That is just not fun. Exercising, there are some forms I like and others that . . .

STEVE: You don't go there.

ETHAN: It's shocking, really. If you do under four kilometres of jogging there is supposedly less pain.

STEVE (jokingly): They say you can gain an extra 10 years on your life by exercising, meditating, having a good diet and so on. But you would have taken ten years off your life by jogging, meditating, and all that other stuff! As long as you have that conflict that says, *It's not fun*, you're never going to do it. Who does like exercise? You are a great exerciser, right, Lee?

LEE: The exercises that I choose to do; I don't do it if I don't like it. I love exercise but I choose exercises that I find fun.

MATT: I go running every day.

STEVE: Right. The connection is only inside your mind and your nervous system. It's not in these other people's nervous systems. It's not just in your mind and your nervous system, but in your energy system.

JANE: I like exercising but I enjoy making myself do it because I think that it's worth it. I like the way it makes me feel afterwards, how well I feel, and how much more energised. I'm motivated by the end results of exercising.

STEVE: You are focusing on the end results whereas he's focusing on what it's going to be like doing it. That's why you go out to exercise, because you're connected to the feeling of what it's going to feel like after you've done it. He's connected to the feeling of pain that's going to be involved in doing it.

ETHAN: The funny thing is, when I play the drums, after two hours of playing drums, I'm absolutely knackered. I'm sweating. I

165

feel like I've run five kilometres. The other guys are up there playing their guitars. It's hard work.

STEVE: Some people would call that exercise.

ETHAN: Yeah. So I don't know... Is that a form of exercise I'm having fun with?

STEVE: (Humorously) No! It doesn't qualify. Actually, it is. Of course, it is.

Simple Polarity Process

There are several exercises you can do on values. This one I'm going to do right now is for when you've got two conflicting choices. Whenever you're thinking, *Am I going to do this or am I going to do that? Is this more important or is that more important?*

The way to do this is to tune into one of the options and do the tapping on the thoughts energy and emotion associated with that. Then tune into the other one and do the tapping on the thoughts energy and emotion associated with that side. Then do it interchangeably. It's a process for resolving opposites and it works very, very well.

Workshop Example:

JAMES: I see a great risk in heading for abundance for some reason. I don't know why.

STEVE: Okay, so with James's values, the way he's wired up is that security is more important than abundance for him. Therefore, you don't go for abundance, you go for security. That, therefore, suppresses the desires and the energy that you have for creating abundance. It stops you from being able to manifest those things. Is that correct, James?

JAMES: Pretty well.

STEVE: What's the change that you'd like to make?

JAMES: I would just like to recognise the fact that abundance is what it is. It's there.

STEVE: What if this security need settled down a bit and didn't feel so life threatening or crucial? That would allow it to move a little further down the list naturally and abundance could move up to where it maybe really should be. (To the group) As long as he's driven by the need to have security, he's not going to be easily able to do things that might create abundance.

If you apply tapping to the root emotional experiences behind each of these values, then that is one way of sorting this out. I would go through and ask, *Where did I learn that this is important?* I would then do the tapping on those reference experiences. If that actually is a solid, true core value of yours, then it will stay.

Let's say this security value is here because of experiences you've had where you've learned that it's not a secure world. It's not safe. You need security. There's not enough. All that scarcity-type thinking bound up in those scarcity experiences. Do the tapping on those memories and associations: Number one on the thoughts, number two on the connected feelings, and number three on the experiences where you got the thoughts and connected feelings from, and either it will settle down to a lower position on the list or it will stay where it is. If it does stay in the same position though, it will probably transform. What might end up there is a more solid sense of inner security rather than a grasping, needy, worried insecurity.

When you apply the tapping to a value belief and its associated thoughts, feelings, and experiences you are not trying to *make* it do anything. You may decide intellectually, *I would like security to be down at number five. I would like abundance to be up at number two.* You can say, *I would like number five to be number one. I would like number two to be number ten. I would like number three not to be on the list at all, but it is.* So no matter what you decide intellectually, emotionally is where it's at.

Trevor, where would you want recognition to be on your list?

TREVOR: Certainly it can go down quite a few pegs and I don't think it's necessarily an evil thing. It's just something that's actually getting in the way of other things. It's actually stopping me from doing things. If I am subconsciously asking the question, *Am I going to get recognition for doing this? If not, then I'm not going to try,* then I see that as a negative. If recognition actually comes out of something I do as a natural organic process that comes out of something, then I say that's fine.

STEVE: It can also be a fear that you can get caught up in the recognition and forget about the important stuff.

TREVOR: Exactly. I might actually do something that compromises one of my other values because it gives me recognition. Perhaps a concrete example is where I tend to appease somebody because I want them to like me, but really, it's an assertiveness problem. When what they need is not really for me to like them, they need to be told to get out of my life because they are out of integrity with their behaviour.

DEAN: Just a thought on the recognition thing: I sometimes think maybe ego is not a dirty word. My second value is esteem not to be driven by ego. It should be to be happy in your life and with what you do. Getting recognition can feed your esteem. Basically we all want self-esteem. Sometimes we can get hung up on, *Oh, we shouldn't get recognition. That's just not Australian to do it.* I think sometimes to want some type of recognition in a healthy way is okay.

STEVE: That's okay but that's not the way Trevor sees it. Again, what's hardwired into you? The challenge for you, Trevor, is that, number one, you've discovered that you have been driven by that recognition need. Even if you're getting it, you get to feel bad because you shouldn't need that, according to your beliefs. Even when you're getting what you're driven to need and want because of whatever has happened to you where you've learned that's important, getting that, you should be able to feel successful, but you don't. What a bummer! You're damned if you do and you're damned if you don't. Getting to the point where you're at, Dean, may or may not happen for Trevor. If you treat that need for recognition, you might actually acknowledge it and say, *Okay, I've got a need for recognition. That need for recognition is actually quite healthy and good and it can help me. If I didn't want recognition, I wouldn't even be doing any of these things.*

It settles that negative part of it down potentially. It settles the fear. *Feelings are not bad. It's the toxic, excessive and stuck feelings that we want to release and the good core stuff will still be there.* That's what I believe.

Let's illustrate this with James and then I'm going to give you some exercises to do on your own value system.

James, where did you learn that security is important?

JAMES: At home when I was young.

STEVE: Give me an example.

JAMES: I lived in a very working class neighbourhood. I came from that background where there was a lot of lack.

STEVE: So your experience is of lack. In essence, that's what you've been driven to continue with and you are just replicating that experience in a way. We can get to some of those experiences of lack in a moment. Where did you learn that abundance is important? Where did that come from?

JAMES: I just see it all around me but it's not accessible to me.

STEVE: Yes, so it's over there. The rich people have got it. F. Scott Fitzgerald said *The rich are different to you and me. They have money!* For you, that (abundance) is over there in the distance and this (lack) is here. You're in the lack and they are in the abundance. That's where you want to be. In some ways, your life, in fact, the kid in the lower class home seeing the people over there who have stuff and not having it yourself, that's just a replication of your childhood experience unless you change it.

Here's what we are going to do. We're going to do a polarity exercise with this. Like you say, they are opposite poles.

(To James) You've got security at one end of the spectrum. At the other end of the spectrum, you've got abundance. At the moment, security is positive and abundance is negative. (To the group) In other words, he's more attracted to security. He actually feels more comfortable there than he does with abundance.

JAMES: Yes, that's in terms of feeling.

STEVE: What he'd like is for abundance to be positive and security to be negative. (To James) In fact, part of you feels negative about security and part of you feels positive about abundance. It's just that the predominant charge is the opposite of that at the moment.

JAMES: Yeah, security seems to win most of the time, or all of the time whether I like it or not.

STEVE: The reason why it wins is because it's more important. Security is more important than abundance, not intellectually, but in your emotional and energetic experience.

JAMES: Right.

STEVE: What I want you to come up with is some reasons why security is more important and some reasons why abundance is more important. I can demonstrate this with you and then it will become more obvious how to do this as an exercise.

So for you at the moment security is much more important than abundance. If you don't have security, you don't have a base to go anywhere. If you go outside the boundary, you are unsafe...

What we're getting into here are some of the reasons why security is so important and so we start on that side of the fence and compile all those reasons and argue as strongly as possible for the importance of that value from those perspectives.

Then you can go to the other side and you can argue for the opposing value. You can say abundance is more important than security because...

JAMES: It gives me more freedom. And ultimately security.

STEVE: Exactly. Your security needs would be taken care of if you had abundance. However, when you say that now, what thought comes up in your mind?

JAMES: The opposite.

STEVE: The opposite one does. This is a positive-negative exercise. I'm going to start with what's the most positive at the moment for him even though maybe on an intellectual level it shouldn't be positive. I'm going to say security is number one because emotionally this is true for him.

(Steve and James conduct tapping whilst focusing on the following statements which were drawn out from James):

Security is number one and I need security more than abundance.
Security equals safety, and without it I'll be unsafe.
I have to look out for my security needs.
Security is more important.
Security is crucial.
If I don't have security, I'll have insecurity and I can't handle insecurity.
I need security.
I need to stay secure.

STEVE: Take a deep breath. What thoughts are coming up in your mind?

JAMES: Yeah, that's all true.

STEVE: So it feels true for him. At the moment, it is actually quite solid and therefore, it's not going to budge from one single round of tapping. For the sake of the exercise, let's go over to the abundance side. Now we're going to say abundance is number one. That's not true for him but it's what he *wants* to be true. When you're doing tapping on this, one thing you have to understand about this is that tapping is actually working on the negative associations and attachments. For James, his goal of abundance is a negative emotionally. *His goal of what he really wants in his life and what he really wants to become is currently negative to him.* If the negativity of that doesn't settle down, then he's not going to go for it.

Tapping on this can actually feel excruciating.

(Steve and James conduct tapping whilst focusing on the following):

Abundance is number one.
With abundance I don't even have to worry about security.
Abundance is actually the reality.
Abundance is most important to me.
I can have abundance.
I want to be abundant.

STEVE: Take a deep breath and check in.

When you are in that lower class environment, you have part of you that doesn't even accept that you want to become like those other people. Does that fit for you, James? It did for me. I was a 'Balga boy': *We don't ever want to be like those snobs.*

JAMES: It's not my place.

STEVE: No. Start tapping and say, *Abundance is my place and I can have abundance and abundance just is. Abundance is most important. Abundance is. I am abundant. I can realise my abundance. I accept that abundance is important to me. Abundance is much more important than security. With abundance, I don't even have to worry about that stuff.* Take a deep breath.

What feelings does that lead you into?

JAMES: What came up is: "That's not true."

STEVE: Isn't that funny? You do the so-called positive thinking and the person goes to the negative. You do the negative thinking and the person goes to the positive. It's quite bizarre. So now what we've got is two opposite ways of thinking and we're going to put them together and see what happens to them.

We're going to just work interchangeably now on security and abundance. Keep tapping as we do.

JAMES: Can we change the word security to safety?

STEVE: Safety is really at the core of what security is about for you, isn't it? The feeling is that if you go for abundance, you're unsafe, right? Abundance is unsafe. Security is safe. There's the positive of it. It is the negative of abundance. The positive of abundance is?

JAMES: Freedom.

STEVE: The negative of security or safety is?

JAMES: Danger.

STEVE: It's always the people who have the strongest security needs who are most threatened by things that are happening in the world. They don't want anything to change. When people within organisations want to make organisational changes the people who have security as their number one value are usually the first ones who start complaining, resisting, fighting, unionising, and so on.

(Steve and James tap interchangeably on positive and negative sides of this values conflict and start integrating them)

I need to be safe and that's most important
But I would rather be free
But that's not true because then I wouldn't be free I'd be unsafe.
If I go for abundance I'll be unsafe.
If I go for security, I'll be unsafe.
Security equals safety.
Abundance equals safety.
Security is most important.
Abundance is more important.
That's not true.
If I don't have security, I won't be able to do anything.
If I don't have abundance, I'm not going to go anywhere.
Abundance is more important.
I need abundance.
I need security.

I need abundance more than security.
I want abundance, but I need security.
I need abundance, but I want security.
Abundance is security.
Security is abundance.
Security is the key to abundance.
Abundance will give me all the security I'll ever need.
That's not safe.
Abundance is totally safe.
There is no such thing as total safety.
Security provides safety.
That's a myth.
Only abundance will give me safety.

STEVE: Take a deep breath.

We're actually just interchanging the ideas and therefore the emotions attached to them. Interchangeably security is going to win and interchangeably abundance is going to win. You've got two opposite ideas and you want to ultimately hold them both at the same time. The key is to realise that these are not intellectual ideas, they have strong emotions attached, and that's what is being tuned into as well. How you are thinking *and* feeling about them is being affected by the other in that moment, if that makes sense.

James, how do you feel about abundance right this second?

JAMES: I have no feeling at all.

STEVE: How do you feel about security right now?

JAMES: Same. Ambivalent.

STEVE: What if I say you need to be secure?

JAMES: Nothing comes up.

STEVE: What if I say if you go for abundance you're going to be unsafe?

JAMES: No. No.

STEVE: You are saying no, but what are you feeling?

JAMES: It's not true.

STEVE: I know it's not true intellectually. I'm interested in what the feeling is.

JAMES: That's the feeling.

STEVE: It doesn't even feel true. It's still processing. This is quite an interesting exercise to do because you've just tuned into something which is jerking you this way and you're tuning into something that's jerking you the opposite way at the same time. You are going like this (oscillating). Is that true?

JAMES: That's true.

STEVE: That's still processing.

(Recommencing tapping after a short pause): Say, *Things were a lot easier in the old days. When we knew what was most important. That is security. If you don't have security, you've got nothing. If you keep focusing on security, you will have none. Abundance means I can have anything I want.* **But** *I can't. Because I'm not one of them. I'm a poor boy. I'm a working class citizen.*

JAMES: That's not true.

STEVE: It *was* true, wasn't it? But it doesn't feel true right now. What feels true right now?

JAMES: I can. I can have it all.

STEVE (humorously and provocatively testing James): Okay, but you don't deserve it!

JAMES: Yes, I do.

STEVE (continues to gently provoke and challenge): The minute you go for it, you're going to be unsafe.

JAMES: That's true pretty well universally anyway. Nothing is totally safe.

STEVE (now agreeing): Exactly, that's the reality. The only real security is the security you find inside yourself.

JAMES: Yeah.

STEVE: That will continue to process for you. So keep tapping to facilitate the ongoing processing.

You can see how doing this starts to interlink and transform the two different ways of thinking. Ultimately what happens is generally the person has themselves down one end of the continuum and if they go through the process, they might settle down and then say, *Okay, now I'm really here* (in the middle of the continuum). If you keep doing this positive-negative process (something Jung calls holding the tension of the opposites), they may go through a period of confusion and ultimately, they can potentially transcend the entire bond.

If you are *attached* to *having* to have abundance, it's only the opposite of security, it's potentially just as much a trap. **We are releasing the emotional attachment to the concept and the entire continuum itself. That's where we're going, and that is ultimate freedom.** That doesn't mean we lose our contact with reality and with the world. You'll still be able to manifest abundance, but you won't *have* to manifest abundance, which is just a security need anyway.

JAMES: Yeah.

STEVE: This exercise we just did is only one of the things that you can do to release some of these emotional attachments. The other thing that you could do, and we could have done, is ask, *Where did you learn that?* We could do the exercise on the legs supporting the table of the belief that security is crucial.

You can just start by focusing on security and do tapping on the belief that security is important. Without security you won't have safety. You need that. Then you can ask, *Where did you learn that 'security is crucial' belief?* If you can get back to one or two of the key events and do tapping on those, you can have a huge shift in how much that drives you or how much you're attached to it.

This simple polarity exercise is about using the opposites and tuning into the opposites and using the tapping to transform the effects of each of them on you. It's really quite powerful.

Summary of How to do the Simple Polarity Process

The way this works is you identify two values which are in

179

conflict. Then go to one side and focus on that value and you 'make that win', meaning you come up with all the arguments for why that value is most important. You then go to the other side to the other value and you 'make that one win'. Then you bring them together and you let them each win interchangeably. Of course you are tapping all the time.

Before you start, it can help to come up with two lists. One will be a list of why this (first value) is important and the other will be a list of why this (second value) is important. You'll then be able to use those things in the tapping exercise. It will be much easier for you to do having them written down in front of you than trying to think of them as you go.

So when you start, tap on the points in any order and as you tap run through the list of all the reasons why that particular value is important. Then when you have finished the first list tap as you run through the list of all the reasons why the other value is important. Then tap and interchangeably focus on the reasons from each of the list, starting with the first item on the first list, then changing to another tapping point whilst focusing on the first item on the other list, then proceed to the second item on the first list, and so on.

Another way to do this is to start by tapping on any reason why the first value is important, and then move to another tapping point and focus on a counterpoint to that reason and / or a reason why the second value is more important. And so on. Keep doing this until you experience a shift or until you have gone through each of the lists and then stop, take a deep breath, and check how you feel. If there is still emotional intensity you can continue the process.

If as you are going through any of the reasons from either list you become aware of a past event or strong feeling or some other aspect comes up, focus your tapping on that until the intensity reduces and then continue with the process.

Using the Simple Polarity Process for Decision Making and Resolving Conflict

You can **use this for any conflict** where you are being pulled two different ways.

Let's say you had to make a career choice and you didn't know which way to go. Shall I go for this job or shall I go for that job? Part of you thinks the first option will be great for you and part of you thinks the second option will be great for you. Option 1 will lead you to something good and option 2 will lead onto something else, which is also good. And maybe there are potential downsides to each choice as well, so you can't really decide. Actually you can, using this process.

You start by saying, *All right. This (option 1) is the way to go. I need to do this (option 1) for these reasons ... and you focus on each of the reasons in turn.* Do the tapping the whole time while you're doing this. Then you go the other way and you totally go with the other option: *I need to do that (option 2) for these reasons... and then you outline all the good reasons why option 2 would be great.* You totally go with it. Sometimes just doing this process will settle things down and you'll see what's clear. If you still aren't clear, you put them together interchangeably and ultimately after a period of tapping while you do this either you'll work out, *This is the way to go. This is right for me. I know it because it feels right.* Or, you may come up with a third alternative which is better, a way of integrating the two together or a way of doing something that is better than either of them.

DEAN: In the context of my fitness, one of my health values which I think is high on the list. I've got to identify what is preventing me from being healthy.

STEVE: Let's put it this way: Assuming that you keep putting achievement as more important than your health, what's going to happen? Ultimately just based on what you're saying, if you put health higher, then you'll be able to achieve more because you'll have health and ongoing longevity. It will all work together in that way. At the moment it's not working because health keeps getting put aside.

When you do this in a workshop setting, often people in the group connect with other people's issues and benefit from that. This is the great value of doing this in a group. One person will be doing the work and other people will be getting benefits whilst tapping along. *You can also get helped on other issues that appear to have nothing to do with another person's issue.* Gary Craig called this process borrowing benefits, whereby when someone is tapping on an issue of their own in front of a group others in the group who tap along will often experience benefits on issues of their own that may not be related to that presenting issue.

In this process, while the other person is working you are tapping but you're not thinking about your issue. You're just tapping along. At the end of that time, when we have everybody go back to the issue that they thought of originally and see how that feels now, often as much as 80% of workshop participants report a significant shift on that issue without even thinking about it while they were doing the tapping.

Being Specific vs. Energy Toning

JOHN: Wouldn't that suggest that tapping in itself is a beneficial process any time?

STEVE: Of course it is. Tapping works when you are being very specific. Tapping can also work as a general energy toning process without any need of specific focusing at all. If you just do a lot of tapping during the day, without specifically focusing on any particular problem or issue, you'll get results. I would suggest that that's a good idea for almost everyone. I suggest to most of my clients one or two sessions a week where you sit down for 15 or 20 minutes and really do something specific. The rest of the time, just tap throughout the day whenever you can. Five minutes here, ten minutes there, three minutes over here... Also tap for first aid when things happen that upset you. When things bring up feelings for you, you can tap to settle those feelings down. You can also tap 'mindlessly' for an hour while watching television or whatever you're doing and the benefits will accumulate in your nervous system and your energy system.

You can also link tapping to your other regular habits and things you do each day so the tapping itself becomes a habit. This is a form of emotional fitness. It's a healthy addiction.

CHAPTER 9

Resolving Values Conflicts Using the Detailed Polarity Process

There are three main ways that you can have conflicts in your values:

One is that the value can have a conflict within itself where you can have a value of wanting security, which is our particular secure feeling at that value, is held in place by insecure feelings that are antithetical to you getting what you want and those are the insecure feelings that have been hardwired into your nervous system by your past negative experiences. In fact they are driving the need for security now.

Secondly you can have conflicts between different values on your list such as the classic conflict between freedom and security; this is a conflict between seeming opposites, as discussed in the previous chapter example

Then you can also have a third type where you have a value that you really want such as you want to achieve but then you have a negative away-from value—a feeling that you don't want—which is very strong, the feelings that you want to avoid such as rejection.

Workshop Demonstration:

In this demonstration I start with the **Simple Polarity Process** then proceed on to a more **Detailed Polarity Process** for resolving values conflicts. In this more detailed approach we identify all the different emotional associations to each value, both positive and negative, allowing you to release these emotional hooks and attain a higher perspective.

ROWENA: Is that why you would self-sabotage if you have two values that are completely different? So if I value achievement but I also value acceptance and being part of the group is that why I would do that?

STEVE: Exactly, because if you go out and achieve too much you are going to get rejection and not acceptance.

ROWENA: I think that's exactly what happens and it just clicked to me.

STEVE: You have part of you pulling this way and part of you pulling that way. This is why I came up with the concept of 100% YES! Because most people when they talk about their goals and where they're heading or what they really want it is a yes-no. It's an 'I'd like that, *but...*' It's not a yes at all. 100% YES! is like when you were a kid and you really love ice cream and your parents say, '*Do you want have an ice cream?*' and you scream '*YES!*' or maybe you love going to the beach and they say, '*Do you want to go to the beach?* and you excitedly scream '*YES!*' You are all in, no parts of you are holding back.

So, Rowena, do you want to work with this?

ROWENA: Yes.

STEVE: Start tapping. Now tell me about the values conflict that you'd like to work on.

ROWENA: I'd like to work on the achievement and acceptance one because I think that goes back to when I was bullied in primary school. I was wanting to be part of the group but I really want to achieve, I would like to achieve a lot more.

STEVE: Okay, so which one is stronger, the strongest one for you right now, which one is higher in terms of being drawn to it right now: achieving or acceptance?

ROWENA: I'm conflicted because I'm stuck in both because I am in my own business and I'm trying to get out there and I pull myself back as soon as I put myself out there and someone makes a comment. I find myself doing something ridiculous to take myself straight back.

STEVE: So which one is higher right now?

ROWENA: Probably achieving.

STEVE: Okay, so achieving is on the left side of the page and on the other side would put what seems like the opposite which is acceptance or gaining acceptance.

ROWENA: Yes, staying within that normal group.

STEVE: I will go to do this in two parts: we are going to do it as an exercise and in the first part, the first level is a more simplistic level and even though it's simpler and can have a deep result, you may have to do the second part which is a bit more involved in terms of how you put this together.

The first part is to start tapping on the strongest value which in this case is achieving. So, ROWENA, start tapping and repeat after me:

Achieving is important.
I need to achieve.
I've got to achieve more.
Achieving is more important than acceptance.
If I could get over my acceptance fears I could achieve a lot.
Achieving is number one.
I need to achieve more.

Okay, take a deep breath.

What are your feelings, thoughts, reactions?

ROWENA: Well, I believe that. I believe I can achieve more, that's what I want to be able to do but I've been scared of going there.

STEVE: Okay, and your fear of going there is what, that you are not going to have acceptance?

ROWENA: Yes, you don't want rejection and so you don't go out there.

STEVE: (to group) Okay, so funnily enough by going with that side and tapping on the importance of achieving she is getting more in touch with the other side, so now we can go to that side which is actually the less strong energy. If we went there in the beginning (to the side of acceptance) there would be a repellent perfect towards achieving being more important to her.

(To ROWENA) Okay, so start tapping and repeat these things after me:

I need acceptance.
I shouldn't do but I do.
I'd like to be accepted.
I need to be accepted.
I want people to accept me.

And what's happening when you say that?

ROWENA: Yeah, I feel that need to be accepted, to be part of the group.

STEVE: Yeah, (indicates for ROWENA to repeat along)

I've got to be part of the group.
And if I push my head out too far it might get chopped off.
So I need to stay down and be accepted.
Stick with the group.
Be part of it.
Not get rejected.

Okay, take a deep breath. And what's happening now?

ROWENA: I feel quite calm about it. I know I want to be a part of it. I do throw myself out there because leadership is quite strong for me but I'll take myself back as soon as I start to feel threatened.

I don't feel I have that strength yet to stand out there and take it all and just say this is who I am this is what I want to do...

STEVE: Okay, now that we've tapped on each side in turn now we discover play both sides interchangeably and see what happens.

Start tapping and say:

I need to achieve.
But that's not true, I really need to be accepted.
I wish I didn't, actually I don't, achieving is more important than acceptance.
Acceptance is more important than achieving.
I wish I believe that but I don't.
I'd rather achieve than be accepted.
I'd rather be accepted than achieve.
I need to achieve.
I need to be accepted more.
Acceptance is important.
Achieving is more important.
Acceptance is where it's at.
If I'm not accepted there is no point achieving anything.
I want / have to be accepted so much.
I want to achieve what I want.
But that's not true, I'd rather be accepted.

Okay, take a deep breath.

(To group) This is the reality of the way we think often where we're pulled this way and that...What's happening to you Rowena?

ROWENA: That would be true, that's the way I think often: back and forth.

STEVE: So right now what's happening in your body?

ROWENA: My body is quite calm. I also feel quite warm in the fact that I know that's a huge challenge for me.

STEVE: I'm thinking that the calmness is good because generally these things are going to evoke strong feelings. What we're doing is we are tuning into each and settling each down in turn and then we are focusing on the dilemma, the push / pull, and toning it down with the tapping. Now this is the simple starting point for the exercise.

Here's what to do:

Identify two values on your list to try this on. If they have an obvious conflict then that's great; if you can't choose two that have an obvious conflict then look at your values list and see if there's one that is higher than you want it to be and / or one that is lower than you want it to be and choose that to work on. For a higher one consider which other values might be keeping it up there or for a lower one what are the values that might be keeping it from going up higher and then you can do the exercise by contrasting those two values.

Ultimately you can choose any two values from your list to do this exercise with and you can still have some potentially very good outcomes come from that, so they don't necessarily have to be obviously in conflict. If you do have two values that are clearly in conflict it can be easier to do this exercise but you can choose to do this with any two values because they are all connected together and they all work together to help you to get what you want.

A participant in one of my workshops did this exercise with love and joy because for her love was not a positive—her experience of love was that people die and therefore for her love did not include joy.

In this exercise when I do it I am not really trying to make one side win and make the other side lose, in fact I'm aiming to help the person be released from their current win / lose configuration. The way this is currently set up in your nervous system and in your beliefs is that not only is one better than the other but that that one needs to win at the expense of the other. And this means that part of you wins while part of you loses. But what about the legitimate parts of you that need that, for whatever reason? If you find a way to help these parts that are pushing and pulling each other away to be integrated without having to constantly have an internal turmoil then you can have a much more happy and successful life overall.

For example, with one workshop participant who I'll call Olivia, she had a conflict between the pull to be responsible and the pull to achieve. She would feel guilt when she was achieving and also feel guilt when she was doing the responsible thing. There are parts of her that want to be responsible, and parts of her that want to be 'irresponsible'; parts that want to achieve and parts that want to not achieve. When I say parts I mean that there are emotional hooks to do each of these at the moment. After this exercise and particularly the extended exercise that we are going to do now, the full polarity process, this emotional intensity settled down and she saw that it was possible to have both.

Detailed Polarity Process

Let's return to the workshop example where I demonstrate this extended process with ROWENA on her conflict between achieving and acceptance.

At this point, we have Rowena's higher value achieving on the left-hand side of the page and the lower value acceptance on the right-hand side of the page. Now we draw a line across the middle of the page and another line down the middle of the page, making four quadrants. I then question Rowena and place her answers into each of the four quadrants as you will see in the diagram at the end of this segment (Page208).

STEVE: So, ROWENA, what does achieving give you? What are the positives of achieving?

ROWENA: It gives me self-worth. My mum will be proud of me. My family is proud of me. (It means) I've done something with my life. I don't want to leave this world not having achieved something.

(Steve writes each of these in the top left quadrant)

STEVE: Excellent, good. Now let's look at acceptance, what's the positive of acceptance?

ROWENA: I think I've always felt outside of the group and I see how much fun that they have on the inside of the group and I have been there occasionally and I realise how good it is to be in that group...

STEVE: Okay, so that's the positive of acceptance. (writes this in top right hand quadrant) Acceptance means you get to be in the group rather than outside the group. But in a negative sense you've felt like you're outside. (writes 'I'm outside' in bottom left quadrant) What else is good about acceptance?

ROWENA: No one is going to try to knock you down. If they accept you you feel secure and loved and not threatened. You can feel the love in the group and there is support...

STEVE: You feel the love!

ROWENA: Yes.

STEVE: Okay. And the problems, the negatives of having acceptance (points to left hand bottom quadrant) or needing acceptance is that you are still feeling like you're outside of the group; what is the negative of that, what is the cost of that for you?

ROWENA: The cost of it is that I will underachieve, I'll bring myself back, and I know I'm doing it but I still do it...

STEVE: You bring yourself back, you hold yourself back...

ROWENA: Yes.

STEVE: And what are the negatives of achieving, if there are any? (indicating to left-hand bottom quadrant) I say if there are any because some people will have trouble identifying any negatives to their high positive value. For example, in my case, what could be negative about my number one value of love? Except for the fact that I were not so needy about it; that is negative. And if I'm like *love love love love love* and don't do anything else my family won't be able to get rid of me. So (to Rowena) what are the costs of achieving? And maybe the costs of achieving at all costs?

ROWENA: I think you become a little bit too focused so you can become selfish.

STEVE: Okay, so you don't care so much about other people and what they want.

ROWENA: And you don't have the love and acceptance from them because you're being selfish to them.

STEVE: And you end up alone?

ROWENA: You feel isolated, I guess, when you're out there.

STEVE: Yes, you could be too far out there and you're so far away from the group that you can't even see them.

ROWENA: They don't understand where you're at.

STEVE: Okay, so what we have done here is we have mapped out the two sides to each value: what each value gives you and what it costs you. Everything has a benefit and everything has a cost, so if you're going for achievement it could cost you some relationships or some connection and some acceptance. Going for acceptance could cost you some achievement.

So now we can play with this and we want to start with the strongest one, the one with the strongest energy, so we start in quadrant one which is what the highest value gives you; in Rowena's case, what achieving gives her. And then we move to each of the other quadrants in turn. We're starting with the strongest energy and belief which says achieving is good (quadrant 1) and needing acceptance is bad (quadrant 3). Then we will move to quadrant 2 (what acceptance gives), then to quadrant 4 (what achieving costs), then we will go "all over the place". But as we go we are going to check in. Rowena?

ROWENA: I think I've always been one of those people that has to keep it together, I have to be strong, but I don't think it allows me to release that energy too easily in front of other people even though I cry easily.

STEVE: So let's tap on that which is what you're aware of right now. (to group) It's more important to start where you are at than it is to do this process perfectly. So let's just tap on whatever you're aware of *first*, whether thoughts or feelings; what are you aware of at the moment?

ROWENA: At the moment I feel just a little nervous.

STEVE: Okay so start tapping and say:

I'm a bit nervous.
I might get emotional.
I'm worried about getting emotional.

So what's happening now? ...

ROWENA: It's probably a bit stronger, I'm more nervous about mucking it up or not doing it right.

STEVE: Ah, that's the fear behind the nervousness, that you might not do it perfectly?

ROWENA: (nodding)

196

STEVE: Okay, so now that we found the thing that triggers the emotion we're going to focus on that and tap ... So just tap and say:

I've gotta do this perfectly.
I've gotta get this right.
I've gotta do this right.

Now put your attention on the feeling, what's happening?

ROWENA: It's calming down, it's okay to make a mistake now.

STEVE: (Gently provoking, with a smile) No, it's not! (Rowena smiles)

(To Rowena) Okay, let's play with this. (motioning to the board. Starts reading from the first quadrant, while Rowena repeats and taps)

I need to achieve.
Achieving gives me self-worth.
It makes my mum proud and I want to make my family proud.
I want to make my mum proud and I want to make my family proud.
I want to feel like I've done something ... with my life.
Achieving is important.
I like to achieve.
I want to achieve more.
Achieving is where it's at.

Okay take a deep breath...

What's happening with that, what's the feeling?

ROWENA: It makes me feel quite powerful.

STEVE: Okay, so that's the good side of achieving for you. Now let's go down here. (quadrant 2, negative side of acceptance)

Tap and say:

But I need acceptance and that's annoying because then I underachieve.
And if I go for acceptance I'm not going to achieve as much.
I'm to be held back.
I'm not to make Mum proud.
I'm not having a great self-worth.
I'm just gonna be hooked on acceptance.
And I do want to be hooked on acceptance.

Take a deep breath...

Okay, what's happening there?

ROWENA: That actually makes me feel quite sad...That makes me feel sad that I do that to myself.

STEVE: That you hold yourself back in that way? (Rowena nods) Okay, let's do some tapping on that sad feeling, where is that feeling in the body?

ROWENA: In my tummy.

STEVE: Okay, just put your hand there on your tummy and tap with the other hand and we are just putting our focus on that feeling in your tummy. (To group and to you, the reader) When you have a feeling you are *in the zone*, there is no need at that point to keep going on to doing all the other parts and pieces of the exercise...If you've tuned into a significant feeling then tapping and staying there for a while is good place to be. (Keeps tapping with Rowena in silence for a minute)

ROWENA: Yeah, that's good.

STEVE: Okay, so now let's just move over here (top right hand quadrant, quadrant 3, what acceptance gives Rowena) and tap and say:

But I'd like to be included.
I want to be part of the group.
If I'm part of a group I can feel secure.
I won't be threatened.
I'll be safe.
I'll be included.
And I'll be one of them.
And I won't be sticking my neck out.
And I won't be too different.
And they'll love me.
And I'll feel the love.
I want acceptance.
Acceptance could be good .
I could do with a bit more acceptance.

ROWENA: I could do with a LOT more acceptance!

STEVE: (laughs, continues the process, Rowena repeating along)

I like acceptance.
I liked being accepted.
I want to be accepted.

Take a deep breath. Okay, what's happening with this one?

ROWENA: The same thing, it's definitely what I want and I feel powerful with those statements. I do want to do that ummmm...

STEVE: Do you hear that 'but'?

ROWENA: (laughs) But I don't know how I can bring the two together.

STEVE: (provocatively exaggerating) Well, you can't bring them together, they're opposites! In your mind in your system, that's the 'truth' for you...

So there is a yes for this, yes, I'd like that but I can't have both...At the moment there is a disparity. When you say the feeling, Rowena, does that cause you to have good feelings?

ROWENA: It's being part of the group that made me feel good.

STEVE: All right, let's go down here now, (indicating bottom left quadrant number 4, costs of achieving) so now that we have done that last bit it's easier to go here. If you went straight here at the beginning there would be a repellent effect.

(To ROWENA) So just tap and say:

If I achieve at all costs I won't be accepted.
And anyway it's a bit selfish to want to do what I want.
I do not feel isolated, not included in the group.
I would be so far above people that they wouldn't even understand me.
And they wouldn't accept me.
So achieving too much could be a problem.
And I'd be isolated.
And that wouldn't be fun at all.

Okay, take a deep breath. Okay, what's the feeling for this one?

ROWENA: That definitely brings me down...It doesn't make me sad, but it brings me... it's like it's taken the fun out of it. I'm not sad like you would be if someone died but I don't have any joy left inside me...

STEVE: It sucks the energy out?

ROWENA: Yeah, it sucks all the energy out.

STEVE: Okay, so let's do some tapping on that feeling of the energy all being sucked out. And again all we do is focusing on now and that feeling. (Both Steve and Rowena tap in silence for a few moments)

ROWENA: That's definitely made me feel a lot calmer, like the sapping energy is gone and I just feel back to myself.

STEVE: Okay, so let's go for a ride...

(Indicating that they are now going to proceed through all the quadrants interchangeably and mixing things up)

So start tapping and say:

I need to achieve.
Achieving is the best thing.
But it costs me acceptance.
I need to be accepted.
I want to be accepted.
But it costs me achieving.
I'm really underachieving because I need acceptance too much.
I'm under accepted because I'm achieving too much.

Acceptance is good.
Except when it isn't.
Achieving is good.
But then you miss out on acceptance.
Achieving gives me self-worth.
Acceptance make me secure.
I need to achieve.
I need acceptance more.
I don't need acceptance.
I do need acceptance.
I'm underachieving.
I'm under accepting.
I need more acceptance.
But I'd rather have achievement.
But achievement costs too much.
And it's insecure.
Acceptance is secure.
Achieving is good for my self-worth.

Okay, take a deep breath.

(To the group and to the reader while waiting for Rowena to integrate that tapping) I'm just trying to go interchangeably here. And if you want when you are doing this you can just read from the list and take one from each in turn, but when I do this with a person I'm trying to also notice and tune into their ongoing experiencing.

(To Rowena) What's happening right now?

ROWENA: I have an unsure feeling I'm not confident which way to go because I believe in both...So I'm not sure which one's going to be more important.

STEVE: That is often a first step for this that some people go into confusion, and some get a bit disoriented, it's like they are being jerked in two different directions at the same time, they can end up a little bit dizzy and they are questioning what they thought was true, they are considering all kinds of new possibilities. So when you are doing this just be aware that this can happen and take it gently and do it at your own pace. (To Rowena) It's a fairly mild form for you at the moment.

ROWENA: Yeah, I don't know which one (is more important) now ... I know I sacrifice for each at different times but do I give up one for the strength of the other or do I focus on one and ignore the other, or...?

STEVE: Let's play with that...Let's play with those different thoughts... (Tapping together)

Achieving has to win.
Accepting has to win.
I need to be more into achievement.
Because achieving gives me self-worth.
It'll make Mum proud.
It'll make my family proud.
It'll show I've done something.
But it'll make me unaccepted.
Which is insecure.
If I had acceptance I'd be secure.
Acceptance is not threatening.
Lack of acceptance is threatening.
Acceptance is feeling the love.

Acceptance is not achieving.
I want to achieve not be accepted.
I want to be accepted not achieve.
I can't have acceptance and achievement.
I have to achieve or be accepted.
I have to accept or be achieving.
And acceptance is more important.
But acceptance costs me.
I underachieve if I concentrate on acceptance.
But if I focus on achieving I'm under accepted.
I want to be accepted.
I'd rather achieve.
Acceptance is where it's at.
Achievement is better.
Overachieving is bad for me.
Underachieving is bad for me.
Over-acceptance is bad for me.
Under-acceptance is bad for me.
I can't have acceptance and achieve.
I can't achieve and have acceptance.
Acceptance and achievement are different.

Take a deep breath...(To the group) So I'm trying to go with her belief that they are so different. (To Rowena) All right, what's happening?

ROWENA: I feel good about that because at the end of it right before the last couple of phrases I thought, why can't I have both?

STEVE: (Provoking to test) Well, for good reasons...

ROWENA: I *can* have both.

STEVE: (Continues provoking to test the strength of the change) Since when?

ROWENA: Since I decided! (Both laugh)

STEVE: (To group) So this is another stage that happens for a lot of people. Again, I'm not trying to make one value win, I'm not try to make them integrate, I'm just trying to tune into each side and when I'm tuning into each side I want to speak the truth of that as she sees it...So when I go over here (quadrant 1: positives of achieving and what achieving gives Rowena), I want to be yes for Mum being proud and family being proud is good, and when I'm going over here (quadrant 3: positives of acceptance) I'm going to be yes to acceptance is secure and so on. This is why it is really important if you do this process with someone else to really tune into their real reasons. And if you're doing it with yourself then allow yourself to go there and argue fully for each side.

You can use this process for any situation whether you have an either / or going on or you think I don't know whether I want this or that. And you can do it by going, okay, here's why I want this and why this is better followed by here's why I want that and why that is better; here is why this would be good and here's why this would be bad, here's why that would be good and here's why that would be bad. And you are tapping the whole time to help those feelings to integrate. And this is what I'm aiming to do with Rowena, I'm going to let her sort herself out when the emotion start to shift and release the attachments to this.

It's not really an attachment to achieving or an attachment to acceptance, it's actually attachment to a duality. And sometimes people have themselves at a particular point on the continuum between these two extremes and after tapping they sort their priorities out and realise they can be somewhere in the middle; other people realise they have been overbalanced on one side and they now have permission to explore the other side...And other people realise that there can be integration...They discover they don't have to be stuck with either / or, and that they can have both, or there is another alternative or a series of alternatives which arises which is better and which encompasses both of these. And still other people rise above the entire belief system and realise that it's all bull***t! That is actually enlightenment! Or at least the first stage of that; most of us are still dealing with pain / pleasure attachments, that's what most of our life is made up of at the moment. But by progressively tuning into some of these emotional attachments and tapping it frees them up a little bit more so you're free to see things differently and to feel differently about them.

(To Rowena) We might just try one more round just for fun... (Rowena nods)

Just say (while tapping):

Achieving is the best.
But acceptance is better.
I need achieving so I can have better self-worth.
But I'll feel better if I'm accepted.
So acceptance is more important.
But acceptance makes me underachieve.
Achieving is selfish.
But it's good for my family.
It makes me feel good.
But I would feel good if I was more secure.

In the acceptance of other people.
But that would make me underachieve.
And would hold me back.
I Want To Achieve I Don't Want To Be Held Back.
I want to be accepted.
But I'd only accepted too much.
Coz that would constrain me.
I don't want to achieve too much.
Coz then I'd end up isolated.
I have to achieve and accept at just the right level.
I need to be part of the group.
I will be out on my own.
That's a bit selfish.
I really want to be included.
I need the self-worth of people accepting me.
I need the self-worth of achievement.
I need the security of acceptance.
I need the security of achieving.
Achieving too much is isolating.
Being accepted too much is underachieving.

Take a deep breath.

I'm not feeling too many strong negative emotions from you right now.

ROWENA: Yeah, I'm not feeling any strong feelings either way.

STEVE: (To group) It's like she's moved on, I'm not sensing a big charge on it.

ROWENA: (Motioning to the board) That described exactly what was going on in my mind before I got here.

STEVE: So what's happening in your mind right now?

ROWENA: It's kinda calm, I'm not bothered by it, it's not evoking any negative feelings either way...

STEVE: Okay, we're going to pause the exercise here, a round of applause for our volunteer.

Ok, not it's your turn to do the exercise. Complete a similar chart for two of your values that are in conflict, list the positives and negatives you associate to each, and start tapping through each of elements in each of the quadrants!

Rowena's Polarity Process Chart:

ACHIEVING	ACCEPTANCE
1. Gives / Why it's good	3. Gives / Why it's good
• Gives me a strong sense of self-worth • Mum / my family will be proud of me • I'll feel I've done something with my life	• I'd be in the group • Feel secure, loved, not threatened • You don't get knocked down • You feel the love
4. Costs / Why it's bad	2. Costs / Why it's bad
• Become selfish • Feel isolated • I'm outside the group • They don't understand you	• Underachieve • Hold / bring myself back • Low self-worth

Here's what's great about this exercise: You can do it completely wrong and still get a good result. The main thing is just to do tapping on one side and then the opposite. Just doing that will often take you somewhere really good.

Feedback From the Workshop After This Exercise

TREVOR: With Tim, on the one side was adventure and exploration and on the other side was stability and the feeling of being settled in. We worked on the adventure side with no problem at all. As soon as we started working on stability, he almost had steam coming out of his ears. It was a real hook, a real issue for him.

STEVE: Yes, there's part of him that wants to settle in and have stability, but a huge, massive part of him that also says, *No, don't go here. This is bad. You will die!*

These inner values conflicts have ramifications in many areas of our lives and when you conduct the polarity process on them you can then free up energy for different behaviours and responses in those areas.

JENNY: My conflict was hard work versus fun. What I noticed, what came up first was really not so much the good of hard work and the bad of fun. It was more the possibility of not working hard and having fun was far more challenging. That's where all the emotional stuff came up. For me, my definition of fun is actually wherein lies the problem. It's how I define fun. I define fun as being silly, potentially embarrassing. The thought of being embarrassed and looking like an idiot is not an option.

STEVE: Underneath that is the fear that you're going to end up being embarrassed?

JENNY: That's what came up. It was a huge fear of being stupid. It was a huge issue. That really all welled up. That one overpowering emotion drives all of that.

JENNY: Dean said to me, *What about being on stage?* I'm like, *I'm cool with that so long as there's no possibility of me making an idiot of myself. As long as I'm in control and I can look good.*

STEVE: I'd be willing to bet that there were some significant experiences you had where you were humiliated, embarrassed in public and the connection was made between you having fun and that humiliation. If you now go back and treat that memory, you might be able to free up the ability to have fun where that isn't going to happen. Even if it does, it doesn't have the same effect on you because you're no longer that kid.

JENNY: It always leads to the hard work because my brother and sister were twins. I was three. I wanted to work harder by doing chores.

STEVE: What about you, Dean?

DEAN: Mine was health versus achievement. I had an emotional shift when I'm talking about health and energy and clarity of mind. I felt the energy and I felt the clarity of mind, it was quite amazing.

STEVE: Well, tomorrow morning, when you get up to jog, it may or may not be there, because jogging itself is still associated with pain, but being healthy and maybe thinking about health isn't as painful now for you. That's guaranteed to have a shift on your choices because now if health doesn't feel so bad, there's no barrier to engaging in healthy behaviours. There's not a strong internal objection that says no to that.

TREVOR: For me, it's almost like a revelation, like these lights going on that I hadn't seen before. I'm trying to be the perfect father (but) it's an exercise in futility. In doing that, I am trying to extrapolate from that and be the perfect businessman. Those two are just never going to work. I've got to have a good, hard look at some of this stuff.

STEVE: If you can allow yourself to be an imperfect father and an imperfect businessman, you might get better at both.

TREVOR: That's right. I might be better at both. For the moment, I'm beating myself up. When I'm trying to be a perfect father, I'm compromising my business. When I'm trying to be a perfect businessman, I feel that I'm compromising my fatherhood. I'm never going to win that battle.

STEVE: It is a paradox. Actually, sometimes being an imperfect father can allow you to be a more perfect businessman. Sometimes being an imperfect businessman can allow you to be a more perfect father.

TREVOR: It would be cracker if you could be both and be fine.

STEVE: If it's worth doing, it's worth doing badly.

I was working with a professional golfer the other day and he's doing the PGA right now. And when he came in to see me he already had mapped out how he was going to fail. He was saying, *Okay, this is what I always do. I get to the about the 27th hole and then I stuff it.*

I started exploring with him and I questioned this. He said, *Oh, I'm just being realistic.* I said, *You're not realistic. You're not considering all the possibilities. Why aren't you stuffing it up earlier? That's being realistic too isn't it?* He said, *Well, it's not realistic because I don't stuff it up earlier because there are good reasons why I don't stuff it up earlier because of the way I approach it.*

I said, *You know what? You could deliberately go out and make a mistake so that you don't have to. What happens if you play bad on the first few holes?* He said, *I'll definitely make it up on the next few holes.* I said, *Well, that's the way to go then.* He said, *Gee, now that I don't have to worry about making a mistake, I feel like I can go out there and just play the game.*

All the pressure was off him about making a mistake. No golfer is going to play golf on any given day without making a mistake. It just doesn't happen. If there's an area where perfection is impossible to achieve, it's golf. Even the person who's had their most perfect round ever has had a couple of holes that were not so good or a couple of strokes that were relative shockers but then they recovered because they did a good shot next or on the next few holes. That's just the way golf is. It's the same in parenting, it's impossible to be perfect.

When you give yourself permission to be imperfect, you'll release a lot of tension and unleash a lot of energy that is bound up in that internal conflict.

Now, you may be thinking, "Oh, my gosh. I've got a lot of stuff to work on. I've got a lot of emotional baggage." The good news is that you don't have to address this all in one go. Even a bit of tapping work applied to a key values conflict and the underlying beliefs, emotional attachments and past events associated with those values is going to open up a lot more possibility and a lot more expansiveness than you had before.

Now, Dean, just the fact that you feel differently about health allows you to look at things that you wouldn't have been able to look at before. *Your reticular activating system (your brain's filtering system) opens up and allows you to see other options and possibilities that you wouldn't have noticed before.*

Now the feeling isn't bad about those things. You have a more attractive force towards things that are going to feed that positive value and the things that were in the way are not there as much.

How to Go Deeper With This Process

Some people have very strong values due to particularly hurtful experiences in their past. In this case you may have a lot more work to do in order to create lasting shifts in emotion and behaviour. If you conduct the polarity process on a values conflict and you feel like you haven't moved very much on that, ask yourself the same questions we applied earlier to negative beliefs: *Where did I learn that this is important? Where did I learn that this is SO important?* Ask this for each of the values involved and then do some tapping on the events with negative emotional intensity.

You can also simply work through your values list and apply this process of looking at the significant emotional events where you learned that value was important and applying the tapping process to those events which have a lot of negative emotional intensity.

I would encourage you to do this at the very least with your top two or three values. Take a few moments now and apply this process to your number one value; you'll be glad you did. I consider the values work I did in applying tapping to my number one value of love and the experiences in my past where I learned that love was so important (many of which were experiences of lack and where I wasn't feeling loved at all) to be some of the most profoundly helpful and life changing of all the self-development work I have done.

When you do this process of applying tapping to the conflicts and blocks which are preventing you from experiencing your important values, you'll discover like I did that what you've been seeking is actually already here, right in front of you.

I applied this process on love which is my most important value and, for the first time ever after this, I felt love in a really deep and profound way. It's always been important to me that my wife and kids know I love them and that they know they are loved. Really, however, underneath that it's been important for me that *I* feel loved. For example, I always used to say to my wife, *Why don't you tell me that you love me? You should be telling me that you love me.* Of course, she's done a million things to show me that she loves me, but was she telling me? No. So I would admonish her, "You've got to tell me!" She'd respond gruffly, "All right, I love you." Then my response would be, "You've got to say it like you mean it. You've got to say it in a loving way." And instead of the love I wanted it would end in an argument.

As soon as I started doing some tapping work on my not feeling loved and feeling unloved in the past (which by the way is probably what drove love to become my number one value) the more I started to realise and feel the love that was already there all the time but I wasn't able to recognise it and feel and experience it before. When I was young much of the time I didn't feel loved by my parents but I know they loved me intensely. They weren't doing the things that I thought meant love, but they were doing many things that I know now were loving all the time. I just wasn't getting it, and more to the point I wasn't feeling it. I know now in retrospect that some of the problem was that they were *showing* me in various ways that they love me and I wasn't seeing it because I wanted to *hear* it. So this was a problem in some ways of a different communicational style and preference.

Now, my eyes are a little more wide open and I've started to both see love and experience it. I had a wonderful experience on my birthday when I turned 42, just after having done some tapping on my memories of feeling unloved as a child. I was in bed in the morning of my birthday with my wife Louise and all the kids came in. They gave me a beautiful photo book with pictures of the family and the stuff that we've done together with some special photos of each of them and some little funny, quirky statements next to each. It was full of wonderful photos of them so that when I go away I've always got something to remind me of my family. Louise said, "Josh (my eldest) was up all night typing the things on the computer." Olivia, said, "We should cook Dad breakfast in bed."And my son Callum was jumping on top of me saying, "I love my daddy. I love my daddy."

And that was the first time that it all really got through to me. At that moment I was filled with feelings of love like I'd never felt before. Tears started streaming down my face from the sheer joy of that moment, and they didn't stop for about 45 minutes.

The thing was I now know that my wife and kids had been doing stuff like this all the time, but I never actually felt it and allowed it in until after I did that work on releasing some of the feelings of *not* being loved. I couldn't see it or experience it until I got rid of the baggage and the blocks that were in the way.

The minute you let this stuff go, it just is. It's just there.

I now believe that we are surrounded by what we want all the time, but our inner conflicts and beliefs can stop us from seeing it, accessing it, and allowing ourselves to experience it.

CHAPTER 10

Goal Setting

Now we're going to look at your goals. If you've done some work on your values and clarified what's really important to you, the goals that you set now will be much more meaningful. I always say that there is no meaningful goal setting without values clarification, meaning that your goals should help you to achieve and live your values. If they don't, then you could spend your entire life climbing the ladder of success and find its been leaning against the wrong wall (I wish I could remember who first said that). Or you achieve your goal but it doesn't give you what you really want.

When you decide to set a new goal, your internal barriers and conflicts and unconscious blocks will be triggered and rise up automatically.

In fact, **if you want to discover what your unconscious blocks are, there are three main ways:**

1. Get into a relationship. Your partner will trigger your unconscious blocks on a daily basis.

2. Think about the irritating habits of others. The things that irritate you in others represent disowned parts of yourself.

3. Set yourself a big goal. The minute you do that, you will provoke / invoke all the objections and the reasons why you can't have that and the reasons why that is impossible for you and so on. These are the negative beliefs you have learned from your past experiences and most if not all of them are false.

I believe that one of the purposes of setting goals is to manifest those parts of us that have been suppressed, those parts of us that want to be healed, and those parts of us that want to expand and be and come out into the world. So when you set a goal it is really about self-expansion.

Your goal might be in the area of financial abundance. The minute you set that goal, you're likely to get some tension, or constriction, which is actually the opposite of expansion and the opposite of abundance. As long as that feeling is associated with your financial goal, then you will be pushing against your own energy system and nervous system to achieve it. The constriction may be coming from unconscious blocking beliefs about what you can do and what you can't do. It may be coming from a specific belief about money. It may also be coming from a conflict in your values that needs working out. Whichever it is, you can use tapping to treat it and free up your energy and your capacity to act.

Ultimately, whether we're working on goals or we're working on values, we're actually working on the same thing.

Now we're going to work through a goal-setting process which will be different to anything you've done before because this time it will include the power of tapping to release the attachment to your unconscious blocking beliefs.

Setting Goals

When you have clarified your values and what's most important to you (which you have done if you completed the previous exercises), then the real secret to success is to live your values and spend most of your time, money and energy on the things that are really most important. What we want to do is to move on to setting goals that will enable you to realise your highest values.

So far in this book, you've done some work on your values and unlocked a couple of the major conflicts by applying tapping to them and you have hopefully, reduced some of their emotional intensity. *Now that you've done that, you can go through a goal-setting process and you should find the goals you set will be different; they will be more centred on your true values.*

Goals are about what we want and values are what we think that is going to give us, i.e. values are what we *really want* from achieving our goals. So values are crucial in helping us define which of our goals are most important and in particular which are most important now.

When people set goals they ask can I have *everything* I want? Maybe, but you almost certainly can't have everything you want *at the same time.* Do I believe you can have *anything* you want? Pretty much, yes, I do. But can you have *everything* you want? Well, why would you want to?

The process of being alive is to a certain extent a continual process of coming up with *more* things that you want and coming up with more ways of expanding and improving. We seemingly have an endless list of wants. The key is to work out which of those are worthwhile, which are worthy of you, and, if you like, which will give you 'the most bang for your buck' in terms of giving you what you really want in your life.

Now that we are going to consider your goals, it's important to review the concept of the big rocks and **it's important that your goals ensure that you get those big rocks into your life, otherwise your goals will mean nothing and won't bring you the fulfilment that you want.** Unless your goals reflect your true values, you are not going to get what you want. This is also called prioritising. Just like values, not all goals are equal. You may want a lot of things but you don't want them all equally, and some will give you more of what you want than others.

Jim Rohn says in every area of life there are only a few things that make the most difference. If you find out what the few things are that make the most difference and you focus on those, then you leverage everything you do. What are the things that make the most difference in your life, your career, your relationship, your business? If you focus on them and you make sure they are in there, then everything else is going to be cream. You'll guarantee that you are getting the important things into your life.

You are going to fill your life up with a lot of things, a lot of stuff. There are going to be millions of things that you want. There are going to be thousands of them that you are going to get. The question is, are the ones that you get going to be the most important ones and the ones that actually make the most significant difference for you and the ones that you really want? Or are they going to be lots of little things that you thought you wanted or that seemed important at the time?

Robert Allen says the reason why most of us are not successful is that we give up what we ultimately want for what we want right now. The challenge is putting those big rocks in that we ultimately want and even allowing ourselves to think we can have them.

I think one of the main uses of tapping is to release those barriers to being able to have those things, to *release the emotional barriers and attachments that stop us from being able to go for those bigger things that are more meaningful, that are higher quality.*

What is that for you? What are the things that make the most difference for you? Those are the things that you want to focus on. The few things that make the most difference.

Now we're going to move into a process of goal setting. The minute I even mention this, some of you are going to have a negative reaction! And that is where we need to start tapping, even before we start to set some goals.

Let's Look at What Happens in the Workshop When I Mention Goals:

STEVE: What's your reaction John?

JOHN: It's not going to be good.

STEVE: It's not going to be good. I'll suggest why for you just knowing the little bit about you. What happens is if you set goals now you have a bunch of other jobs to do. Is that correct?

JOHN: Yes. You have plans.

STEVE: I did a workshop in Singapore once and the minute I mentioned goal setting, one lady just literally collapsed in her chair. She went into a total slump. Why? Because for her, every time she sets another goal, she now has more things that she has to do. Her list of burdens and responsibilities gets larger. To me, however, goals should be about what you want, not what you don't want. **How about setting a goal for things to be lighter and easier rather than harder?** The key is the feeling it gives you. If you don't like planning and goal setting to you, John, means planning then it gives you some of the bad feelings that you feel about planning. Until you change this feeling you're not going to want to move forward and set goals. And that's what tapping is for.

And what's your reaction?

JOHN: Just that how am I going to choose?

STEVE: How to choose. Whatever your issue is that comes up, this is something to apply the SET tapping to.

The minute you sit down to the goal-setting process whether you are conscious of it or not, some objections will be there. They may come up as thoughts or as feelings, or more unconsciously in a tendency to procrastinate or do other things which ultimately thwart your intentions. The objections may be limiting what you will do and preventing you from doing it with your full power. In John's case, it will make him want to run from the room and not necessarily do it.

JOHN: Yes.

So here's the solution: The minute you want to set a new goal or change things in any way do some SET tapping on the objections first. Another term for the objections, or what's behind them, is limiting beliefs. They might come up in the form of thoughts that say, *I am not good enough, I don't deserve it, I'm not good at planning, Goal setting doesn't work (or, goal setting doesn't work for me), I don't know what I want.* The objections might come up for some of you as particular feelings or body sensations, such as a tightness or tension or butterflies, or as emotions such as fear, anxiety, or a sense of foreboding. Whatever your objections are and whatever form they come in, do some tapping on those immediately before you go any further.

Another reason to do some tapping at the start is to help to get yourself into an expansive state. Most people approach goal setting through a constricted view. They don't actually consider everything that is available to them. We will often only consider the things that we will allow ourselves, i.e. what we think we deserve. When you do the goal-setting process in this book, I want you to allow yourself to consider all possibilities. But for most of us when we start all possibilities are not available to us as far as we are concerned. That's because we've learned that there are limits to what we can have, to what we are allowed to have, to what we deserve to have, to what we are capable of, and so on. That is, our beliefs become like a constricting box within which we live.

How Your Assumptions Can Limit Your Results

I love the nine-dots puzzle. It's a classic logic puzzle which illustrates the effects of our limiting beliefs and assumptions on our performance and our ability to solve problems.

The task, which is illustrated in the diagram below, is to connect the nine dots using four straight lines without lifting your pen from the page. Only about 5% of people will solve this problem on their own; most have to be shown what to do. Even if you have seen it before and think you know the answer, I have a challenge for you so please stay with me here.

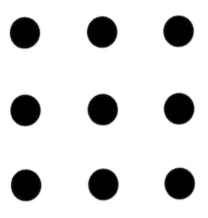

Joining all nine dots basically means you draw lines to connect them. You must draw four straight lines without lifting your pen or pencil (or other writing implement) from the page.

This problem is the origin of the oft-quoted admonition to *think outside the box* or *think outside the square* because in order to solve it you've got to go outside the boundary.

The boundary in this case is an arbitrary boundary which doesn't actually exist in reality. Most people when faced with this nine-dot diagram tend to create a boundary like a square around the edges.

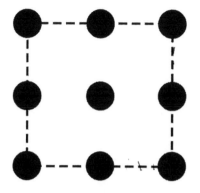

As long as you assume that this puzzle has to be solved by staying inside that square, you can't solve it. The minute you challenge the assumptions and you go outside them, then it becomes possible to solve. Have you found the solution? You'll find it over the page but please have a go first to see if you can solve it.

This happens in one way or another with every single task you approach in life. Everything you set out to do, you approach with a set of assumptions. Your assumptions then dictate what you can and can't do. If you challenge those assumptions and break out of them, then you are empowered to do and achieve more.

But solving the puzzle isn't the only challenge. The challenge is that when most people learn how to solve it with four straight lines they stop. Robert Kiyosaki says this is because we have been taught in school to stop once we find the *one right answer*. However, in business and life your success often depends on finding more than one right answer and / or on finding answers that are better. So once you have solved the nine-dots puzzle using four straight lines, why not now ask yourself *how do I solve it using three straight lines?* It's possible and the solution is given over the page. Try it first before you check.

Here's the solution using 4 lines:

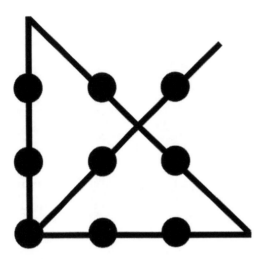

Challenging your assumptions in this way is equivalent to saying in any area of your life where you have a problem to solve, *How can I / we solve this problem in a way which is easier? How can I / we do this at less cost? How can I / we reach more people? How can I / we make it more fun? How can I / we do it more efficiently?* Unless you ask these sorts of questions you stay stuck with the one 'right answer' which may not be right at all in the sense that there will always be something that could be better.

So how do you solve this puzzle with three straight lines? Here is one way of doing it:

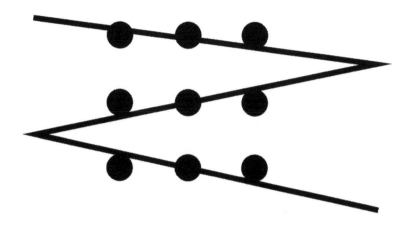

Once you solve the puzzle with three lines, then why not ask, *How can I solve it with two lines?* In fact, you can go even further. You can ask, *How can I solve it with one straight line?*

What's the most obvious way to do this? Well if you got a paintbrush and wiped it across all 9 dots you could join them all using one straight line! In this way you challenge the assumption that you need to use a pen. However, there are also plenty of ways to solve it with one straight line using a normal pen or pencil.

An example is if you fold the lines, and if you fold down the middle of each row, then you can draw one line across the middle and connect all the dots.

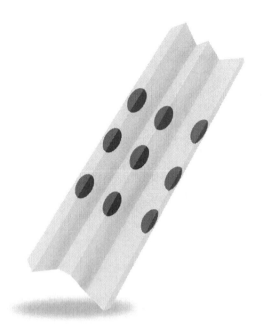

How else can you do it? You could go around the earth three times, each time connecting to a row of three dots on the way on a very slight angle so that each time round then you connect with the next row of three dots in turn until you have connected them all. That may not be a very efficient solution, however, and takes a great deal of energy and effort when the problem can be solved by staying in the room. This is the way some people run their lives. They solve the problem but they've got to go around the world three times in order to solve it.

Is there a way to do this without having to go around the world three times? Yeah, you could cut the dots, put them in a line and draw a line through them. You could also cut them, put them on top of each other and push the pen through them. You can fold them onto each other then draw one straight line.

About 25 years ago I gave this challenge to a group of teenagers and once they started to get creative and challenge the assumptions they came up with nine different ways of solving the problem using one straight line only! I can't remember all of those different ways but the one I like the best and to me the one which is the most efficient is where you curve the paper and draw one line all the way around (see diagram). You don't have to go all the way around the world three times, you can solve it right here using what you have.

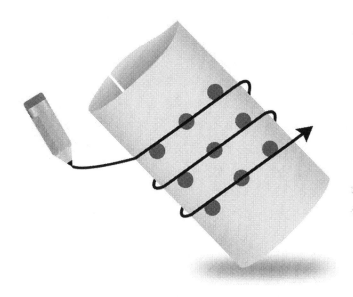

Once you've solved the puzzle with one line, why wouldn't you then say, *How can I solve it without any lines?* How could you do that? You could fold them all into a point so that they are all touching, and therefore all joined. You could cut the dots out and put them all together. Set fire to it and they will all be joined. Some people would say, *They are already connected because they are*

all dots. Some people would say, *They are already connected because they are all on the same plane.* Some people would say, *They are already connected because everything is already interconnected. All separation is an illusion.*

Okay, this may be getting a bit too metaphysical; however, the point of this exercise is to realise that the minute you start questioning your assumptions, then you free up possibilities. Suddenly problems which couldn't be solved a moment ago can be solved. The other main point is to realise that we are all doing this in life without even realising it, boxing ourselves into smaller lives than might otherwise be possible for us.

When my son, Joshua, was just a little baby, we were walking along with him in a pram and a woman came along and said, *Ah, they are really beautiful at this age. Then they start getting worse and worse, and they never get better.* I thought to myself, *Wow! That is your life. That's not going to be our life.* And it hasn't been. You don't want to get infected by someone else's beliefs systems, their limiting assumptions. Their assumptions cause their results and dictate the way their life goes.

Another time, my wife and I were driving home one day after visiting with an old friend. By way of background, this guy was someone who always thought of relationships and marriage as a prison. He was never going to get married and always mocked others who did, but finally he met his match and ended up a married man. However, he was now in a marriage that was the nightmare he'd always said it would be. It was a prison and it was constricting, and it certainly wasn't much fun to be in. If you asked my friend, he'd say that's the way all marriages are. Actually, he'd created it because that's what he expected and that's what he believes. Then he acts 'as if' it is true, and for him it is.

Anyway, as we were driving home, I was talking with my wife about this guy and his wife, how it was literally as if they were stuck in a box. I said, *We've probably all got our own boxes that we are stuck in.* Our eldest son, Joshua, who was sitting in the back of the car interjected, *I'm not. I never get stuck in a box.* I responded, *Oh, yeah? Why not?* He said, *Because I just keep asking questions so I never get stuck.* And I thought to myself, *You're a smart little so-and-so, aren't you!* You see, he's right! He's asking questions. He's challenging assumptions. He's looking outside the box. That means he's not going to be constrained in those same ways that many of us are. It's a great skill to have.

Unless we are doing something to challenge our assumptions and looking for ways to expand, then we stay stuck within our boxes. To me, tapping is the most wonderful tool because without having to actually fight against our beliefs and assumptions which are boxing us in and which can have strong emotions supporting them, you can just use tapping to release the emotional attachments and you'll automatically start to see things in new ways.

The minute you start to feel like you are constricted or that you don't have options, start tapping. And do the same when you want to expand. The minute you think, *Okay, I'm going to set some goals and do some planning,* and your insides go, *Oh, no way!* then start tapping. The minute you start thinking, *I can't decide what to do,* start tapping instantly on that thought and its attendant feelings. You will start to release your emotional attachments to the ideas which are constricting you.

Let's do this. What's your first objection to goal setting?

Here's some more responses when I've asked this question in my live workshops:

JACOB: Getting it right. I've got to get it right.

STEVE: Okay, start tapping, and say:

I've got to get it right and I'm probably going to get it wrong,
I have before and I'm going to again.
This is another opportunity to fail and I don't want to do that, I want to avoid it.
I hate goal setting.
Goal setting is making a rod for my own back.
I might get it wrong.
If I set goals, they have to be the exact ones I want.
I don't want to fail.

Take a deep breath. (Jacob is looking much more relaxed)

JOANN: I had a little bit of anxiety that came up during that.

STEVE: So that obviously resonates for you. What's the thought that goes with that anxiety?

JOANN: It's committing to the goals.

STEVE: Okay, so then you're stuck. Let's do some tapping on that stuck thinking and feeling:

The minute I make a goal, I'm going to be stuck.
I might be stuck on the wrong track.
I don't want to commit.

I hate committing to things I want.
So I ultimately don't want it.
I've wasted all that time, all that effort, all that money, all my energy.
I don't want to get it wrong.
I can't commit. If I commit, I'll be stuck.
I might make the wrong choice.
I'll lose all my other options.
Making decisions limits your choices.
I don't want to limit myself.

Now take a deep breath.

Real freedom includes the freedom to commit as well as not commit, doesn't it? Teenagers often get into this kind of rebellion where they just want to do the opposite of what their parents want them to do. Well that's not freedom. The new definition of maturity—and I learned this from Frank Farrelly—is doing what's good for you even if your parents approve!

How's your anxiety feeling?

JOANN: Yeah, better. I just realised what came up when I was tapping before was about not staying with it until the end—like seeing the goals through to the end.

STEVE (humorously provoking): Well, you won't see it through, surely? You're not that kind of person, are you? So let's go a bit further on those aspects.

Here's what we tapped on next for Joann:

I'm not that kind of person.
I won't follow through.

What's the point setting a goal in the first place?

By this time next week I will have done nothing.

This is a futile exercise.

I can't get myself to follow through.

I don't have enough discipline.

I'm not disciplined.

I'm too lazy.

I won't follow through.

I'm not that kind of person.

There is no point in setting a goal if I'm not going to do it.

There is no point in setting a goal unless I know definitely that I am going to do it.

Take a deep breath. How do you feel now?

JOANN: Really good, I have the sense that maybe this time it can be different. I'm curious to find out.

STEVE: Okay, so we've now been able to open up some new possibilities by releasing some of the attachment to those blocking thoughts.

Almost everybody wants to know before they set the goal that they are definitely going to succeed, that's why a lot of people are holding back. In fact, that's the biggest challenge with goals, the fact that there's *no guarantees,* and the massive doubt that comes up and the fear that maybe you won't get there. In fact, if that doubt isn't there to some extent, then I don't think the goal is worthwhile. That's what makes it exciting, that you don't know for certain what is going to happen!

My First Really Big Goal

When I got my first full-time job I received my first ever tax return and I had the thought, *I've always wanted to travel. I want to travel to America.* I was also motivated to study with Frank Farrelly and he offered a training week in his practice in Madison Wisconsin. So I thought, *We could go over there for a holiday and on the way back I could study with Frank.* So I said to my wife Louise, *Let's go to America next year.* She said, *Great!*

The next day, however, Louise came to me and said, *I've been looking at things and we can't afford to go to America next year?* I said, *Why not?* She said, *Well, here's how much money we've got (not very much). Here's how much money we need (a lot!). I've worked out that if we save everything we can possibly save from our wages for the next year, here's how much money we're going to have (not enough!).* She then said, *Why don't we go in three, four, or five years when we can afford to do it?* I said, *No, we're not going to do that. This money that we don't know how we're going to find, we will never find unless we decide to go before we have it. We'll never find out how to get that money unless we have to.*

You Don't Have to Know *How* Up Front

There's no need to search for ways to get where you want to go unless you have decided to go for it. Without that you won't awaken any of your creative genius. You won't get any more, learn any more, create any more, until you decide to do something that you currently don't know how you are going to do. You'll then have to find out how to do it and you'll activate your creative imagination to search for ways to do it. The only way you can go beyond where you have been and where you are is to get outside your current comfort zone.

The challenge is that **what's currently uncomfortable has to become comfortable.** It has to become more comfortable going and doing that. The problem is that currently it isn't comfortable, and some of the things you need to do, the thought of doing them is so uncomfortable it's positively repellent. That's why we need a technique like tapping to deal with the massive doubts that this causes. Massive doubt, massive tension, massive anxiety, and so on.

Actually, **I believe the true purpose of setting a goal is to become the sort of person who can resolve this challenge.** You have to access parts of yourself that are not in the world at the moment in order to overcome the barriers to achieving your goal, so that parts of you can come into being that aren't present in the world now, or not very much.

There are parts of you that have been suppressed or disowned, parts of you that haven't been allowed to be expressed. Such as the confident you that already exists in seed form, but isn't out in the world so much now. Or the assertive you. Or whatever it is that will be required to step up in order to do this. Those parts have to come out in order for you to achieve this goal.

That's why Jim Rohn says, *The purpose of the goal is the person you become, not what you get.* Once you achieve that, you can give it all away because it's what you've become that makes the most difference.

Not knowing how they are going to achieve their goal is what stops most people in their tracks. That and the fact that there are no guarantees that you're going to find the way or achieve it. Most people think, *That means I might not get what I want and wouldn't that be disappointing.* In fact, since they've learned that they can't have what they want and they believe it's not possible for them and they don't deserve it anyway, **they've already decided how they're going to fail before they even go there.** Like the golfer who had his failure all mapped out when he came to see me. When he left my office, he had three different scenarios in his mind: the normal one, which had happened before, and another one which I had him go into in detail which was the ideal, or something else. He said, *That's the first time I've actually been able to go through in my mind seeing myself doing it differently.*

The normal scenario is now not the only scenario. Now there are other possibilities in his mind. I'm betting money that the result will actually be something else.

Set Goals From a State of Expansion

In order to set goals effectively, you need to get into an expansive state rather than a constricted state. You want to set your goals from a state of expansion and possibility. There are a couple of main ways to do this. One is, the minute you access the objections, treat them using tapping so that they settle down and then you can think more expansively. Another way is to do a process like a splurge (outlined below) which bypasses your conscious judging mind. This is where you think outside the box of current reality.

You can also fruitfully apply SET to your beliefs about what's possible and about what's possible for you right at the start of your goal-setting process. Then you will have opened up possibilities and released some of the chains that are currently binding you.

The Folly of SMART Goals for the Long Term

Have you heard about SMART goals? It's an acronym which stands for: Simple, Measurable, Achievable, Realistic, and having a Time frame. SMART goals are great for short-term planning, but over the long term they are boring, uninspiring, constricting and limiting! If you are basing your life on SMART goals, that's one of the dumbest things you can do! Think for a moment; you are almost certainly using everyday stuff which even five years ago would have seemed unrealistic and which was science fiction less than 10 years ago!

When I was a teenager, we were watching Maxwell Smart on *Get Smart* with a shoe phone with a dial and that was science fiction at the time. How soon after this was it that we had mobile phones? What about video phones? That was the farthest-out science fiction just a few short years back, yet because someone was thinking outside this box to stuff that is unrealistic and didn't exist right then that's how it came to be. And now even more than this is just around the corner. Already these things which were once science fiction are old technology.

SMART goals do have a place and their place is in the next three, six, nine, twelve, even maybe up to eighteen months. This kind of more realistic thinking is really important for that short- to medium-term planning. However, when you get beyond that, how much can happen? The truth is you actually have no idea. If you do something and continue to build on that over a few years, you can end up somewhere completely different from where you thought you would be through the power of compounding returns (as well as synchronistic quantum leaps!). Einstein himself called compounding the eighth wonder of the world. And when you compound your learnings in an area, your actions in an area, your connections in an area, then you end up somewhere far beyond where even you might have projected that you could be. And that thought ought to be inspiring.

SMART goals are good for limiting yourself to a little bit beyond where you are right now. Long term, unless you get outside the box by thinking more unrealistically, you are going to be stuck with what you've already got and only a little bit more. Most people however, when you ask them what they want, they say they just want a little bit more than they have right now and they reckon they will be set, especially in the area of finances. *Just give me 10-15% more than we've got right now and we'll be all right.* Then what happens? You find 20% more bills!

Be Unrealistic

Let's think unrealistically for a moment. Let's get outside the box. Once again, to do this it can help to first use tapping on the constricted feelings and beliefs you have so that you can be more comfortable to start thinking outside the box, seeing yourself doing bigger and greater things.

Use Your Past Resources of Success

Another way to get yourself into an expansive state is to realise that you already have resources within you; you already have a peak performance state within you where you can think this way and feel this way and all you really need to do is access that. That resides in your past experiences of success and achievement and expansion. All you really need to do is go back to one or more of those experiences and key into it until you can access that feeling.

Let's do that.

What I'd like you to do is to think back to any success that you've had, anything that you've been successful at. The way I want you to think about it is not looking back on it and watching it like a movie. I want you to go back into it as if you're back there feeling it and doing it and having that experience now. Step back into it and feel how it really felt being there. Just let yourself remember and re-experience how that felt when you did that.

Now choose another success that you've had in your life. Cast your mind back to the things that you've done well, the things you've achieved and find something you were successful at, and go back into how that felt. And for each, step inside it as if you're back there re-experiencing it, and doing it right now.

After a few minutes of this with some of your key success memories, open your eyes up and notice how you feel. Some people find this very easy and they quickly get into a peak state. If you find this difficult, you can use SET to help you do this, too. It changes your feeling. In that feeling, you can move forward into a more expansive space.

Those resource feelings are always there, we're just not always paying attention to them or utilising them. We're often caught up in paying attention to what to do next. Tapping into your peak performance state is actually quite easy. Associate to the feelings—associate means step into the picture. Don't just see it as a movie. Step into it and allow yourself to feel it and re-experience it as if you are going through it again now.

When Michael Jordan hit the game-winning shot in his college basketball championship, he said, *In that moment, I knew my future was guaranteed.* There was no difference in hitting the game-winning shot to win the championship in the NBA than hitting a game-winning shot in that college championship in his mind. He said, *In that moment, I knew nobody could ever take that feeling away from me.*

I remember watching him play on television and his team the Chicago Bulls was in the finals. In this game it was very close and in the end, there was 1.6 seconds left on the clock. The Chicago Bulls were two points down. Everyone knows they're going to try to pass the ball to Jordan and if he hits a two-pointer it's a draw and they go into overtime, he hits a three-pointer and the Chicago Bulls win. And since everybody knows they're going to pass to Michael, he was actually being crammed out right out near the half-court line by three opposition players. Why don't they pass it to someone else? He's the only one who can be counted on to hit it. They've only got time to pass it to him. He has to shoot it instantly.

Somehow they get the pass to Jordan and he's just about out near the half-court line. There are three players jumping up in front of him, almost over the top of him. He's falling back and then he releases the ball … and it goes *swoosh*! Straight through the ring, nothing but net. I can't describe the feeling of seeing that; for anybody who has ever played basketball it's incredible to think that someone could do that with that amount of pressure on them. After the game they interviewed Jordan and asked him, *How did you do that?* He said, *Every time I'm in that situation, into my mind come all these memories of all the other times when I've been successful in hitting shots in clutch situations. Then I go out there with that confidence.* In that state, the same state he was in when he made the college-game-winning shot, he was able to perform. One of his great skills was being able to hang onto that state, and more particularly to be able to access it when he needed it. And he accessed it with ease at times like this.

The rest of us have to remind ourselves that we have resource experiences that can reconnect us to peak performance states, at least until it becomes a habit. We may have to use a conscious process a number of times to go back to the success feeling and bring it forward to where we are right now, until it becomes a habit. When you do access that feeling, *that's* the time to go into the goal-setting process.

Focus on Your Ultimate Goals

Now when you look at your goals I want you to consider what you want *ultimately*, not just what you want right now. This is something I'd ask you if you were here now in my office and you walked in with a problem or challenge in sports, business, or life. At some point in our first interview I'd say, *What do you want ultimately? Where do you want to go and where you want to be ultimately with this?* If I was working with you on your business, I might ask, *What kind of business do you want to create ultimately?* Even before that, however, I'd ask, *What kind of life do you want to have? What kind of lifestyle do you want to create, ultimately?* Then I'd help you to design the business that can enable you to have that.

The more that you can get the ultimate picture, the easier it is to access your strong motivation and inspiration and then you can plan back to today. Focus on your ultimate goal(s) and find goals that are inspiring to you.

The Goals Splurge

A goals splurge is a process which you can use to bypass your conscious judging mind and get your ideas and goals out into the world. Manifesting is ultimately about taking things from the world of ideas and bringing them into form.

The way to do a splurge is to use any creative process that works for you to get your ideas and dreams and possibilities and goals from being in your head to being out in the world. So that might mean getting them onto paper or onto a screen, by writing it down, typing it onto a screen, by drawing or painting it, or by saying it, recording it, or sculpting it, making a model, or using any other creative process that you can use that allows you to form an initial representation of the final result.

To do this get yourself into a creative state where you can get ideas out quickly before you have too much time to think about them. The minute you allow yourself to think too much about a goal or idea then you'll be thinking, *I can't do that. That's not possible. How on earth do I think I'm going to do that?* Get the ideas out *before* you start working out how or thinking about whether and worrying about any kind of planning or reality factors. That's why speed of doing this is a factor, it doesn't allow you too much time to think and engage with the judging part of your mind which if it comes out too early will potentially kill your dreams, goals and plans.

As I mentioned it's best if you use a creative process that works for you. If you like to draw you can mind map this, or create a blueprint, or sketch images related to your goal. If you like visual representations but can't draw well you can find images online or in magazines that represent what you want. For me, it works to just list things. The main thing that makes it work is ultimately that you end up with things you really want and in a form that works best for you.

So let's do this!

I'm going to give you 15 minutes to get every single idea that you can come up with of something that you'd want. You can write it. You can draw it. You can put a symbol of it or anything that represents it to you by way of actually getting it out into the world. You can pull together pictures or images. Whatever you choose, the key is to do this quickly and not stop to think. Spend the entire time brainstorming the different things that you want.

Do Have Be

When you do this, think of things you want to do, things you want to have, and also how you want to be, what kind of person you want to be. To make the goals you will set and the ideas you will come up with more meaningful, have a quick look at your values list before you start, and if you're looking for ideas for goals then aim to come up with at least one or two goals or ideas for how you can better live each of your values. Look at your values list and for each value ask yourself, *What can I do that will enable me to get that? What, if I set it as a goal, will allow me to achieve more or experience more of that value? How can I live this value more in my life?*

Don't be hung up on perfection and remember to keep brainstorming and coming up with ideas the whole time as quickly as possible without having to think too much. Remember, too, this is not a list of goals yet, it's just a list of ideas. These ideas may become goals if you decide to bring them into form.

You have 15 minutes. Ready, set, go!

If you have completed your splurge what you will now have is not yet a list of goals but a whole lot of ideas and wishes and dreams and possibilities which may or may not become goals. They don't become goals until you decide to make them real and decide that you will.

When I was a kid, my mum used to say, *If wishes were horses, beggars would ride.* We've all got dreams. Everybody wishes. Sadly, many people think that wishing and hoping is all there is to goal setting, that's why they don't achieve their goals and that's why they have such negative associations to it!

So these wishes, ideas and hopes are not yet goals. The difference between one of the items on your list or pictures on your page and a goal is that a goal is something that you've taken through a decision-making process where you've ended up making a committed decision to realise it.

A lot of people have a lot of fantastic ideas. However, a lot of potentially great ideas are killed by doubt, judgement, and negative thinking. If someone has a good idea and thinks it but doesn't take any action on it then it never becomes real. There's a process involved in taking your current set of ideas and possibilities and working out from which of those things you want and then working further from that the things you really want. Putting your big rocks in first. Then transforming the 'really wants' into goals that you will ultimately realise and manifest in the world.

We Are Surrounded by Infinite Possibility

The reality is that we are constantly, in every moment, surrounded by infinite possibility. Albert Einstein, apparently, had burned on his desk a statement which was along the lines of this: 'All creation waits with eager longing for its revealing through the sons of man.' The point is everything in creation is basically available. And the only way it gets to be manifested is *through us*.

It's only if you decide to manifest that stuff, that we—the rest of the world—will get to benefit from it. It's only if you decide to bring that into being that anything ever happens. Only if you go through a process to take it from just being an idea to something that you're going to really do something about will it make any difference at all.

The first part of this process is actually a prioritising process. You've got to work out what your main priorities are so you can make sure that the goals you set and the ones that you realise are your big rocks.

The few things that make the most difference are made into goals first.

So look through your list and highlight those items that really stand out to you as being really good, ones that inspire you and make you think, *I'd really like that. That would be fantastic.* At this stage it doesn't matter whether you believe it's possible or not. You just need to know if it will be good.

When we do this we're moving from a big list or a lot of items to a medium list, made up of the ones that give you the yes feelings and devote thoughts like, *Yeah, I really want that. I want to do something more with it right now.* Or *That would be really wonderful if I were able to create it.* It doesn't mean that the other items you've recorded won't get a chance, it's just that they aren't the ones that stand out to you right now.

The question at this point is not, *Can I do this?* or *How can I do this?* or whether this is possible. The question is, *Would this be good? Would I like this? Do I want this? If it were possible, would it be good?*

If the answer is yes, just highlight those items somehow. You can mark them or put an asterisk, circle or highlight somehow the ones that you want to do more with right now.

The key here is that the ones were going to transform into goals are going to be ones that you really want.

What we're doing here is an initial filtering process to get from a potentially large list down to a more manageable list of possible goals that will have a little more priority now in your mind or ones that attract you right now. For whatever reason, you're attracted towards doing these first or having these things more urgently.

The Power of a Deadline

Something that really starts to sort the wheat from the chaff, and makes a big difference between knowing whether something is a want, a wish or a dream or a goal, is whether you can say *when*. Until you have set a deadline for something, I don't think it's actually a goal.

I think it was Ken Blanchard who first coined the term that *a goal is a dream with a deadline*. I agree with that. There's a lot of debate about this, by the way. A lot of people who teach goal setting believe that you shouldn't worry about deadlines. My research shows that those who set deadlines for their goals outperform those who don't by a significant margin. Because until you decide *when* you don't really need to do anything at all. And the minute you do decide when then you have a basis for planning and an impetus to act. I'm firmly of the conviction that until you have a deadline, until you can say when, you're probably not going to.

I used to travel regularly to the USA and many groups that I worked with over there I would routinely ask, *How many of you want to visit Australia one day?* Almost every person would put up their hands. Then I'd say, *Okay, leave your hand up if you can tell me when you're going to do it.* Guess how many hands remained in the air? Maybe 3% of the people who had initially put up their hands. Those are the people who I believe who were most likely going to make it. Maybe some of the others will too but I wouldn't be very confident about that. When someone says, *Okay, I'm going to come and we're going to be doing it in June next year,* then you start to believe that it's a goal that they are going to achieve, and not just an idea or something that they'd like.

The minute that you set a deadline there's much more of a commitment involved, although you may experience some tension from doing this, especially if it's a big goal. If you do I suggest you start tapping immediately.

So now let's set some deadlines for the items on your list or the images you've compiled. Go through each of the items you have marked as wants and ones that you would like to do something more about and indicate when you are going to do that by or have that by or be that by.

Do this very quickly. Don't spend too long thinking about. Just indicate next to each item with, when you want to have it or do it or complete it by; in six months' time, one year's time, 10 years' time, by June 30, 2027, whatever.

As you go through this process, you are almost certainly going to have reactions and objections arise. Basically, your limiting beliefs will come right into focus. You are trying to go outside of what is, to something which doesn't exist yet. That creates a certain tension. If you're not going far enough outside current reality and there isn't any tension, I suggest that you're not considering goals that are going to stretch you. Unless your goals give you some of that feeling, then you're sticking with what you already know you can do and staying within your comfort zone. So go back and spend a few minutes and identify something that would be a stretch for you, something that you don't know for sure is going to happen or be achievable, but if you did achieve it then it would be wonderful.

The minute that those objections and resistant feelings come up, that's an opportunity to use SET on them, to start to expand your possibilities and release your attachments to old limiting beliefs.

Here's another workshop example:

What's your reaction, Karen? You said, *I'll never have that* or *I can't have that.*

KAREN: The ones on my list that don't cost any money and the ones that aren't too deep I *can put dates to,* but the ones that are most important to me *I am never going to have.*

STEVE: They are actually never going to happen as long as you keep on in that belief! For you, that's a truth. That's an *is.* Actually, the only way that anything can be any different is when that becomes a *was.* To get there, we start with what is and we tap on what is. Also, we tap on what could be. What could be creates the tension as well.

The same exercise we did before, we can do here. There's a conflict that's been set up here between what is—which is the negative belief—and the future possible goal or what could be. But because of what is, it probably won't be, unless it is changed.

One has a repellent force and the other one has an attractive force. Even though you hate this (current reality), it's actually more comfortable for you than this (desired reality). It's very uncomfortable to think about that. You can use the same positive, negative exercise as before, or you can just focus on the reactions and start tapping and start with what is. What is your belief that you can't have that?

Start tapping and say (beliefs that came up below which we tapped on),

I'll never have that, and that won't happen, I know it.
I know what's happened up until now.
My past is determining my future.
I can only see what has been.

What has been defines what will be.
What I've had before defines what I'll get in the future.
I can't have what I want.
I don't deserve it.
I haven't worked hard enough.
I'll be having too much fun.
Until I work harder, I'm never going to have what I want.

Keep tapping and tell us what's happening with your thoughts and feelings.

KAREN: I am feeling a little bit better. It's just like the truth for me. It doesn't matter how much you want it...

STEVE: Start tapping and say:

I know the truth. It's been decreed. The truth is as I believe and I can prove it. Just watch me. The only eternal truth is hard work for no reward. You know you only get rewarded when you work really hard. I have to work much harder.

I'm actually getting Karen to tap here on her negative belief which is about having to work hard, I'm just exaggerating it a bit. This is something you can do for yourself on some of your negative beliefs. When you have a negative belief, like for example a belief about lack and scarcity, you take that and in your mind create an image in the future of you not having enough. Then exaggerate it. For example: *I will be eating gruel and I will be sitting there with nothing and my stupid quest for abundance will have destroyed everything and we'll be in a hovel and collecting food stamps.* You're exaggerating the negative. It's got a certain truth, but it's not really true either. Nothing about the future can be true because it hasn't happened yet!

The more you exaggerate this, the more you will be able to come back to a more realistic perspective that allows other possibilities. That's not what you have right now; you only have one stuck perspective. You've had experiences that have stuck that to you and those beliefs need to be let go of with tapping. Go to it.

CHAPTER 11

Turning Wishes and Ideas into 100% YES! Goals

What we have done so far in our splurge is to put together a big list or compilation of ideas and dreams, which now needs to become a shorter list of things that you're going to do something about, as in your goals. It doesn't necessarily mean that you're never going to do anything about the others, it just means that we're going to pick some of them that are worth working on and focusing on for now. First.

What's going to help decide this is ultimately going to be your values. Going back to the work on your values and doing that is going to open up possibilities for things to drop through the funnel and be realised and come out into the world.

Anything that's preventing you comes down to your blocking beliefs. If you still have a specific belief about that thing, you may need to treat that. If you have an identity belief that you are not that type of person, you may need to treat that block, whatever the block is that comes up for you related to any of these items that become goals.

What happens when there are two of you and you are married? Obviously, you're going to have personal goals. How do you then form a set of goals that work jointly?

You do this exercise then you get together. And you ultimately end up with my goals, your goals and our goals. I think the best relationships have all three of those. You allow your partner to have goals that are completely different from yours and they go off and do their thing. You support them. You do your thing and they support you. And you work together on the goals that are 'ours'.

It's really challenging, though, to sit down with your partner and do a goal-setting process in the first instance because you are going to be coming from different sets of values. In the beginning it's about what you might lose or what you might miss out on and your fears come up. The fear is if they get what they want, I'm not going to get what I want. There are great opportunities for tapping on that stuff.

If you set out to do a goal-setting process with your partner and negative feelings come up, then you've got some stuff to go and treat with the tapping and then after that you can go at it again. When you go at it again, usually the feelings aren't as intense. Then you'll actually be able to go somewhere and you'll have the joy of going there together.

It's a continual process of working with those two sets of values and not only where they converge, but also where they differ. Where they differ creates conflict and potentially excitement, but also challenge. In the middle of difficulty lies opportunity.

We've gone through and set some deadlines and we've shortened our list of goals to a few major priorities. Did you have some trouble with doing that? Many people do when there is doubt about whether you'll be able to achieve this particular result, or this particular outcome. You need to go through that to the other side which is where your success is, and where you'll start moving and improving and manifesting.

With my big travel goal, after my wife Louise said we can't do that and we decided to go forward anyway and discover how, we started searching for ways we would do that. And pretty soon we manifested a job cleaning offices. We spent six months cleaning offices, and in the middle of winter we both went out in the dark to do that job and arrived home while it was still dark. Then we went and worked all day at our regular jobs. We worked flat out for six months. At times we were really tired. At the end of that time however, we had all the money we needed and we went away and we spent it all! We went to Disney World and New York and Washington, DC and the Grand Canyon. We went to San Francisco. I'll never forget driving away from the Grand Canyon in a hire car and all of a sudden I just got hit with this feeling. I said to Louise, *We're here!* She responded quizzically, *Yeah?* I said, *We're doing it! We're doing what we dreamed of!* And she smiled and said *Yes we are!* It was so fantastic. It just washed over me, this feeling.

After we finished that trip and we came back home I said to Louise, *Let's go to Europe next year. In fact, what if we get an around-the-world ticket and skip over to America on the way back and I'll go and visit Frank again?* And then I added, *But let's do it easier this time.*

Let's find an easier way to do it.

Any challenge like this is the same as the nine-dots puzzle; instead of having to go all the way around the world in order to solve it, let's find an easier way, let's search for an easier way to do this.

I discovered I could apply for a grant which would pay the travel component and my costs during the time I was studying with Frank Farrelly, so I no longer had to find all of that money. I started finding ways like this to make it easier.

Some years later when I developed my skills, I got to the point where I started to present at meetings and workshops. Then I got to the point where people would actually pay my expenses in order to travel to teach them. I was getting to travel and all my expenses were being paid which I thought at that time was great. Then at one point I thought *It's still costing me money because I'm not earning anything while I'm away.* So then I decided I wanted to make a profit. Finally, I thought, *What is my real goal? My real goal is to get paid lots of money to travel all around the world, catch up with my friends, have fun, and make a difference to lots of people.* Then as my family grew I decided that I wanted to be able to take my family with me on some of my trips.

I'm now in the position where I have the option to go to a lot of places in the world and I'm saying, *I don't want to go everywhere.* I'd rather go to a few quality places and also have plenty of time with my family, occasionally taking them with me on trips and to be able to leverage the stuff I do when I'm away so that I have a better experience, I make more of a difference, and I help more people. And if I'm away from my family it's only for a little while and I bring back more for them so everything works together based on my values. So my goals have moved up another level again.

Way back when I set that original goal to travel overseas it seemed so big and challenging, but now the idea of travelling anywhere in the world is fairly easy. What I once just imagined has become what is. At each new step the doubts came up again. When I set my goal to get paid and make a profit from a trip, part of me didn't believe I was going to be able to do that. The doubt was there. The challenge is that each time you set a new goal and you decide to go there, then you have to find out how as you go. And there's no guarantee that you're going to get there. The absolute guarantee, however, is that if you don't decide to go there and you don't do anything about it, you're not going to get there.

There is a Chinese proverb I really like that says, *Man who wait with mouth open for roast duck to fly in, must wait very long time.* My research shows this also applies equally to women!

Before we go any further I want to say that I realise that some of you who are reading this are starting from a very low point. You may feel that you are deep in quicksand and if that's the case your first goal is just to get onto solid ground. Once you are out of the quicksand then you can set a goal to find your way out of the jungle. You might set your sights on a hill in the distance and when you climb that you'll be able to see further. At each step you can apply the same strategies: decide where you want to go, what you want to do, and where you want to be, apply the tapping to your objections and blocking beliefs, put together a basic plan and start at the first step. Then it all comes down to persistence and learning and adjusting as you go. Ultimately, if you continue this process you will be really surprised at where you can end up.

Your Four Most Important Goals

I want you to go through your collection of dreams, wishes, ideas and possible goals now and choose four that you'd like to turn into real goals—because they're still not yet goals in my book. They only become goals when you decide that you're going to manifest them and commit to taking the actions you need to take to make them real. And when you decide when you are going to do them by.

The key for deciding on these 4 goals is of course your highest values, so check in with your values before you do this. If you have also completed the exercises on tapping to sort out values conflicts, this will free you up to be closer to 100% YES! about the goals you choose.

Make sure that at least one of the goals you choose for this step feels more than a little challenging to you. At least one of them should be one that makes you think, *I'd like that but I'm not sure if I can achieve it. I'd like that but I'm not sure if I will be able to get there. I'm not sure if I'm good enough.* Or some equivalent beliefs.

What are your four most important goals as you see it right now? I'm leaving it to you to decide the meaning of *most important*. Just choose four for now.

Remember, this doesn't mean you can't move on later to work on the others. Just pick four of them that you want to work on right now. Then we're going to work on building your commitment to achieving these goals. Commitment is an absolutely crucial thing, as shown in one of my favourite quotes:

Until one is committed, there is hesitancy, the chance to draw back, always ineffectiveness. Concerning all acts of initiative (and creation), there is one elementary truth the ignorance of which kills countless ideas and splendid plans: that the moment one definitely commits oneself, the providence moves too. A whole stream of events issues from the decision, raising in one's favor all manner of unforeseen incidents, meetings and material assistance, which no man could have dreamt would have come his way. I learned a deep respect for one of Goethe's couplets:

> *Whatever you can do or dream you can, begin it.*
> *Boldness has genius, power and magic in it!'*

— W. H. Murray in *The Scottish Himalaya Expedition,* 1951

Let's return to the live workshop where I'll illustrate how you can get to this type of commitment to your most important goals and get closer to being 100% YES!

Workshop Segment:

STEVE: Someone give me an example of one of your goals.

WENDY: I want to get fit.

STEVE: Okay. That's a want at the moment. It's not actually a goal. At some stage, if this is going to happen for you, you'll need to go from that being a want to making it real. Otherwise you go nowhere.

The typical approach to this is to create a positive affirmation where you say, *I am fit.* Then imagine that you are that now. Say, *I am fit* Wendy.

WENDY: (With a pained look on her face): I am fit.

STEVE: Have a look at her face!

One thing I learned in psychology is that repeated exposure to an aversive stimulus will not create a positive result. If you say to yourself, *I'm fit* and you get a bad internal reaction, how is that going to help you? How on earth is it going to connect you to the state of being fit if every time you say, *I'm fit,* you get an *Ugh!* It's not going anywhere except in a negative direction. You say, *I'm fit* but what happens in your head and your body? You get reminded of how you are right now—fat and lazy.

So when Wendy goes through the affirmation or tries to go to the end result, the reality comes up and hits her in the face. The no comes up. There's no yes. In my opinion, using affirmations in this way is useless. In fact it's worse than useless because it takes you in a negative direction instead. It reinforces the reality and the 'is' rather than what you want.

I believe that you (Wendy) are actually still at the wanting stage and you haven't yet made being fit a goal. There's a process you need to go through before you get there. That process is, you have to go through the bridge of willingness to get to the stage of manifestation. In fact there are several steps involved in this.

Levels of Commitment

(i) Wishing: You start out at the lowest level of commitment which is a *wish,* maybe something you dream about, maybe something you'd like. Sure, it would be good but there is no real energy or impetus to do anything about it.

(ii) Wanting: At the next level it becomes a *want.* Now it's a real desire and there's a pull. There's an emotional and energetic attraction. *I want that. That would be good.* There's a certain attractive power to it.

(iii) Planning: Next it maybe becomes something that you *plan* to do. That means you are going to go beyond wishing and even wanting and actually put some effort into working out what to do in order to get there.

(iv) Willingness: Even planning isn't enough to ensure you get your goal. It's only when you are able to say *I will* that you actually have a goal. Once you get to the willingness point, then you can go through that to the realisation of your goal. With some goals, especially the big ones, you need to be willing to do *whatever it takes*; that's the strongest level of willingness. And ultimately, a real committed goal says not only that you will, but also *when* you will do it by. When you get to here, you are much closer to the 100% YES point.

You cannot do the cosmic bypass that everyone's trying to do of simply trying to affirm your way to success by repeating *I am so happy...*statements and expect to get there.

Jim Rohn says, *Affirmation without discipline is the beginning of delusion.* He also says, *Don't chant. Plant.* That's where it's at.

In plain language, it's only something that you're going to do something about that really makes it a goal.

Summary of Levels of commitment:

- I wish ...
- I want ...
- I plan to ...

- I will ...
- I will ... by ...
- It is.

Continuation of Workshop Example with Wendy:

Wendy, you're not going to do something about it because at the moment you haven't even decided that you're going to do it. It's just something that you'd like. That's true, isn't it? Say *I will be fit.*

WENDY: I will be fit.

STEVE: Now when you say that, I'll bet you there's some resistance behind it.

WENDY: Yes.

STEVE: What we want to do is apply tapping to that resistance and get to the point where when you say, *I will be fit*, you don't have that same intense resistance feeling; instead, you have a different feeling.

What we're going to do is an exercise to help you move through these levels. You start at the wishing stage and apply the tapping at that level to any resistance. Then when you have settled down the resistance you go through to the wanting stage, and apply tapping to any resistance at that level. Then go to the planning stage and tap on your resistance to planning and preparation in terms of actual steps you can take towards your goal. Then you go through to the willingness stage. Different people will have different reactions at different points on this continuum, some will very quickly be able to go to through these steps and others will take much longer on one or more of the steps.

STEVE: Just say, *I wish I could be fit.* Just feel how true that feels.

WENDY: I wish I could be fit.

STEVE: (Observing Wendy's reaction) It feels fine. Now say, *I want to be fit.* When you say that, what's the difference in the feeling?

WENDY: There's a bit of tension.

STEVE: There it is. Already tension. Go no further. Stop here and start tapping.

Here's what we tapped on with Wendy:

I want to be fit, but I have this resistance feeling.
I want to be fit, but I can't because I'm too lazy.
I want to be fit but I'm too lazy, and I won't follow through, and I'm undisciplined.
I want to be fit, but I'm not going to do anything about it.
I'd like to be fit if you could get there without having to do anything.
I want to be fit but I'm not going to do anything about it.
I just want the result without the effort.
I want the result without having to do anything about it.
I want to be fit, I just don't want to do anything about it.

At the end of this process take a deep breath. Now check to see how it feels:

Say, *I want to be fit.*

WENDY: I want to be fit.

STEVE: How does that feel?

WENDY: It feels okay.

STEVE: Good, let's go to the next level.

Some of you will spend a lot of time on one level because that level really upsets you. Fine. You're still moving through it but you've got a bit more work to do on that level. Try to identify what the blocking beliefs are there. Ultimately, if you do some tapping on those beliefs and their attendant feelings and you're still not getting through it, you might have to go back to *Where did I learn this blocking belief?* and do some tapping on the past experiences driving the emotional attachments of that belief.

If all that doesn't work for you, then consider doing this process with somebody else.

Once you are fine on a particular level, then we can go onto the next level.

Now Wendy, say, *I plan to get fit.*

WENDY: I plan to get fit.

STEVE: I bet you that brings the feeling up again.

WENDY: Yes.

STEVE: So now we're going to do tapping on *I plan to get fit*, tapping on the objections that come up when Wendy thinks about planning. If we have time, we'll go to the point where she says, *I will get fit* and we'll see how much of that feeling is there.

Now do that process on one of your goals that you're willing to work on to increase your commitment to making it happen.

This process can be a lot of fun, especially when you can feel yourself starting to shift through the levels. What first feels forced starts to feel congruent and possible and real. I have found in doing this process people start to not just think of their goals as out there in the distance, they start to be able to connect with them. They start to think and feel, *Yeah, that's possible.*

All of this can be done by yourself. The challenge is there will be a limit to that. The reason there's a limit is that some of your unconscious blocks are, of course, unconscious.

WENDY: Can you do this in a mirror?

STEVE: Yes. When you're looking yourself in the eye, you'll be able to see whether you really mean it or not, I think that could work for you. I don't know that it would work so much for me, but it might work for you. The process is not so visual for me. For me, it's how I'm saying it that makes the most difference. For you if you can't see the congruency in how you are holding your body, how you are looking into your eyes, you're not going to believe it. It's the same with all these processes; the key is to experiment and use a creative process that works for you. The main key is that it works, even if it seems a little bit different to what works for other people.

When you find an emotional trigger, that's something that's a block for you. Do the tapping on that and then test it. If that trigger doesn't stimulate the same feeling, now you can move on to the next level.

These words, such as *planning, I want this,* they have a significant emotional resonance for a lot of people. The *I will* part, that's usually the most tough. *I will* is a real commitment. If you say, *I will do something*, it's far different than saying, *I'm planning to do it.* That often turns into we planned to do it, but we didn't make it. When you say, *I will,* that cuts off your retreat possibilities.

Note: Some of you will find that a visual image that represents these stronger levels of commitment will work better for you than the words. Again, do what works for you.

There's more work to be done to get to the point where you can say *I will* and that's congruent. Where it feels *100% right* for you and you can congruently say it's a 100% YES!

Helping people achieve their goals and live their values feels right to me. It feels to me like the right thing for me to be doing. It's definitely 100% YES! for me. And my aim is to help you to uncover your 100% YES! so that you can go out into the world as the fullest expression of you, doing what you are here to do.

The biggest part of this process is getting clear on your identity and your values, and then setting your goals based on that. However, when you first set your goals, even if they are based on your core values, you've still got to go through a process to make them real. And a big part of that process involves getting to the point where you can make a real commitment to do what it takes.

You start with your wishes and dreams and any blocks at that point you apply tapping to. Then you move to your wants and apply tapping to that. Then you move to planning. If you have an aversion to planning, you do some tapping on that.

Jack, you also had an issue with planning, didn't you, in regards your business?

JACK: The first time I saw Steve, my main issue was my business planning. I kept asking him how to beat this thing and make a business plan and he wouldn't answer me. I walked away and I thought f*** it. My trading has taken off since then. I didn't have to have a business plan and realising that I didn't have to have one *just liberated me.*

STEVE: Actually, it was the stuck idea of planning you had that was getting in the way. It was the set idea you had about the sort of plan that you *should* have and that sort of plan didn't gel with your major values. Of course there is no such thing as a perfect business plan. Harry Beckwith wrote a book called *Selling the Invisible.* He refers to a magazine that highlighted 50 top business strategic plans and yet, within two years, 33 of those companies had gone downhill. So much for the brilliant business plans. Finding something that's going to work for you is more meaningful.

JACK: Well, the thing I've derived from that is just to let go of the other people's expectations, even my coaches. There was a book I was looking at this morning and it talked about how the plan may suit the teacher but not the student.

STEVE: It's what works for you that you want.

JACK: It's what works for me. I know what works for me and what doesn't.

STEVE: Like Jack, whatever stimulates any intensity for you, if you do tapping on that, when you get through you are probably going to go in the direction of being able to plan more easily. And then you'll either be able to make great plans or realise that you don't need that type of planning you originally thought you needed in order to do what you want to do.

Now this might sound like I am contradicting what I just said but the truth is most big achievements *will* require lots of planning, preparation, training and even hard work. Robert Schuller said *spectacular achievement is always preceded by unspectacular preparation.* Some people have big challenges with their willingness to plan and prepare and train for what they want. Tapping can help you to work through this and firstly determine whether the end point is worth the effort, then secondly, help you to release any false negative emotional associations to planning and preparing.

The next stage beyond planning is willingness: Being willing to say *I will* do this. Not *I wish to,* not just *I want to,* not even *I plan to,* but *I will.* Once you get to willingness, once you move through and release your aversion to planning and your aversion to being willing that really allows you to take off.

That's what this whole thing is about. This is the reason why I run these workshops and seminars and why I wrote this book. To help you to move to the point of being able to go for what you really want 100% without being blocked. That all starts with getting clear on what you want and then setting a definite intention to make it real. It starts with your willingness.

When I get to this stage in my workshops often I share images of things I've done that were once dreams for me. Taking our kids to Disney World was an example of this because it was the fulfilment of a dream. I always wanted to take my kids on a trip overseas and I wanted to take them to Disney World and see the joy on their faces. I still remember their screams of delight on some of the rides and the look of awe on their faces during some of the performances and 3-D and 4-D films. That was a dream for me at one time and now it's something that I've done.

Some people look at this process cynically and say, *You do all that and you only enjoy it for that short time.* No, you don't. Once you do it, you've got it forever. You've got how that feels with you forever. It is the same with an Olympic athlete who strives for many years for the chance of representing their country and winning a medal and when they do so they only have a few seconds on the podium. Or the mountain climber who spends many years training to climb the highest mountain yet only gets to spend a few minutes on the summit. But that feeling is available to them forever. And through the process you become a different person, a person who knows that they have the power to manifest whatever they might imagine.

JACK: That's something that happened for my partner and I when we went on our world trip. I've got stuff in front of my desk that reminds me of that trip. I have got memories: I have got screen savers, pictures, photos. It's never left me and it will never leave me.

STEVE: That's right. All of you have had successes like that. You've just forgotten about them. You need to remember some of those things. In the state of remembering that success, you can move forward to the next thing without the same blocks.

Taking Action

"The greatest gift that extraordinarily successful people have over the

average person is their ability to get themselves to take action."
— Anthony Robbins

The Common Denominator of Success:

Many years ago a guy named E. M. Gray wrote an essay called *The Common Denominator of Success* where he outlined the common feature he'd found when he studied those who'd been successful in his industry. Here's what he came up with:

The successful person has the habit of doing the things failures don't like to do. They don't like doing them either necessarily. But their disliking is subordinated to the strength of their purpose.

The great thing now with techniques like SET tapping is that we can work on the disliking, we can make taking the action and going outside our comfort zone less uncomfortable, we can transform those feelings. However, the key thing here to note is that those people had found something that was important enough to make going outside their comfort zone worthwhile. He defined it as a purpose. For me, it means finding something that fits with your most important values and therefore it is worthy because at its core it will give you what you really want.

Action

The last step in getting to 100% YES! is actually the first step and it's also a continual step because it's the action step. None of this means anything unless you put it into action. The difference that makes the difference is actually doing something that moves you closer to realising your dreams, achieving your important life goals and living your values. And then continuing to take action.

I believe if you've been doing the exercises as you've moved through this book, that a lot of the choices you now make will be automatically in the direction of your true values. The feelings you have will be different. There will also be times where you'll deliberately and consciously do things that you wouldn't have been able to do before. And sometimes you won't even discover this until weeks or months or even years later because the great thing about tapping is that the changes tend to integrate into your life very subtly, gently and effortlessly. Sometimes you may not feel a shift when you are doing tapping but you will know things have changed at a later point when you find yourself taking action without the same emotional reaction or resistance you would have had in the past.

I hope you'll do the tapping and get into action towards the important goals that you identified in the previous exercise. What do you do? You do the first thing first.

First Steps

Take a few minutes now and identify some things you could do in the next 48 hours which will be the first steps towards your goals. Do this for each of the four important goals you identified previously.

The important key here is to make the first thing a very small and very easy thing to do so that you can build on success rather than an impossible first step that is such a big leap that you're supposed to jump the high bar before you consider you've done anything good.

For each of your four goals ask yourself:

What's the smallest *first step* that I could take in the next 24 to 48 hours that will take me towards this goal?

When I set the original goal to go on that first big overseas trip to the USA with Louise, the next day I went to the travel agent and wrote out a cheque for $150 (yes, it was that long ago!) as a deposit. She said, *We don't even have the schedules for next year yet.* I said, *I know. I'm doing this for me. This seals the commitment that we're actually going to go.* I did that and that one step then built the momentum to make the next thing happen, and the next thing, and ultimately the whole thing happen, even though we had no idea at that time how we were going to find the rest of the money. At that time, finding that kind of money was difficult for us. Now it seems quite easy.

What's the first thing for you and what is the first step that *you're* going to take?

Write down some ideas *now* for your first steps.

What's something you can do and will do within the next 48 hours?

Tom Peters and Nancy Austin say, *If you don't do something within the next 72 hours, you ain't going to do anything at all.* I prefer 48 hours. The more you go beyond that the more you potentially lose momentum.

Once you've taken your first step no matter how small, the next challenge is to persist and keep on working through the different levels to build your commitment. As you go, apply tapping to any barriers that come up, whether real or imagined.

For the sake of this exercise we want to identify an *actual step* you are going to take that will either bring this thing closer to you or bring you closer to it.

So what's your first step? Take a moment and identify it now.

Our time together, at least as far as this book, is about to come to an end. I appreciate your willingness to come with me on this journey, and to discover and learn new techniques that you can take forward to improve your life quality. I love to work with people who want to move forward and who are willing to embrace what works and run with it, those who are into developing and improving themselves and manifesting a better future and becoming more of what they can be.

I know if you apply the techniques and work through the process and put it into action that you will be successful and find your own 100% YES. If you use these techniques to get clear on your true values and release any emotional attachments to living those values, set goals based on your values, then get into action to go ahead and make it happen, that your life will change in incredible ways.

Always remember, the main criteria for when something is 100% YES! is that it gives you energy rather than taking it away. If it takes energy away, that doesn't necessarily mean you give up on it. It means you need to do some tapping to work out what's causing that energy to go away, and find out whether this is a real yes for you. If it fits with your major values and the block is just fear and negative beliefs, then I hope you use this process to release your attachments to those limiting beliefs so that you can go for it.

Once you become clear on what you want and get into action to achieve it, the challenges don't stop there of course! The ongoing challenge is how to *persist* in spite of what life throws at you; how you stay the course and manage the curve balls that inevitably appear in the form of unforeseen obstacles, frustrations, pressures, rejections, plateaus, relapses, crises, and so on.

When those challenges do occur, take some time to revisit your values, beliefs and goals, and choose how to respond based on your highest values. When you do, you'll know you are doing the right thing for you even if it's tough. And use tapping as you go to deal with the biggest problem anything can really cause you, which is how it *makes you feel*. When you can handle that, you can handle anything.

I hope you'll put the information in this book into action and use the techniques to release your fears and overcome your limiting beliefs, and to discover and align with your own 100% YES! Even more, I hope you'll share this to enrich the lives of others. When you do, you'll not only be enriching your own life, for in giving we receive, you'll be making the world a better place for us all. So pass it on.

I'd love to keep in touch with you. Please write and let me know how this process has impacted on your life. And if I have the chance to meet you, either 'virtually', via my online programs, or face to face, I'll consider it a privilege.

Have fun. Live well. And when you see what you want ...

Go for it!

ACKNOWLEDGEMENTS

A great number of people helped bring this book to publication, and to refine the concepts and processes behind 100% YES!

My parents gave me the grounding which set me on this path via their support and inspiration, and providing just the right amount of challenges to overcome. I'll always be grateful for the sacrifices they made and the lessons they taught me.

Had I not chanced upon my Dad's copy of Napoleon Hill's *Think and Grow Rich* when I was 17, I shudder to think where I might have ended up. That book gave me the impetus and a strategy to lift myself out of self-imposed failure into a lifetime of studying success.

My early study of psychology introduced me to the work of Carl Rogers, Albert Ellis and William Glaser. Self-help "heroes" included Wayne Dyer, E. James Rohn, and Anthony Robbins, whose teachings I found both inspiring and helpful.

I'll always be deeply grateful to Hank Andrews, my post-graduate psychology supervisor, who encouraged me to embrace cutting edge approaches and challenge the status quo. I was also inspired by Milton H Erickson and Brief Therapy pioneers, most notably Bill O'Hanlon. Then I met Frank Farrelly, and became infected with the 'provocative virus'. Frank spurred in me a lifelong love of using provocation, paradox and open-hearted humour to help people change. Frank was a trusted mentor, teacher, supervisor, and deeply loved second father, who has quite simply been irreplaceable.

Studying Provocative Therapy led me to meet David Lake, who became my best friend and provocative buddy. Our collaboration and friendship over the last 25 years has been extremely valuable on so many levels. David taught me a lot about the value of acceptance in relationships. He was also the key innovator behind much of Simple Energy Techniques (SET) as taught in this book. He's also one of the funniest and most brilliant people I know.

I'm deeply indebted to Gary Craig for his gift of Emotional Freedom Techniques (EFT). Gary's EFT was a revelation: finally I could get the results I came into the field to help my clients achieve. SET is in many ways a simpler version of EFT.

I'm extremely thankful to the many clients and workshop participants who have trusted me to work with them over many years. You have been my teachers, I have grown from being in your presence and I'm deeply grateful to have met you. I especially want to thank participants in my 100% YES!, and Go for It workshops and related programs, some of whom you have "met" in this book.

A special thank you to my great mate Terry Power, whose ongoing friendship and relentless enthusiasm for 100% YES! inspired me to stay the path over these years.

Finally, I want to thank my family: Louise, my darling wife, and Josh, Olivia and Callum, our wonderful children. You have always been the most important part of my life; you are my motivation, and my inspiration. I'm proud of every one of you and I love you.

ABOUT THE AUTHOR

Steve Wells is an international leadership coach and peak performance consultant based in Perth, Western Australia. He has a wealth of experience in helping people from all walks of life to find their passion, solve their problems, live their values, and achieve their meaningful life goals.

Steve regularly consults worldwide with elite athletes and corporate personnel to improve their performance and enhance the performance of their teams. He also conducts unique personal development seminars in over a dozen countries worldwide, and has helped many thousands of people through his programs.

Steve is a pioneer in the emerging field of Energy Psychology. With colleague Dr. David Lake, he developed Simple Energy Techniques (SET) and Provocative Energy Techniques (PET). They have trained many coaches and counsellors worldwide on how to get better results for their clients using these techniques.

Steve was one of the first to apply Energy Techniques to enhance performance with elite athletes and to take tapping into the corporate environment, where it can be used to boost productivity, improve performance, and relieve stress. For 15 years he has presented at the Curtin Centre for Entrepreneurship, with many success stories from corporate clients.

Steve is co-author, with Dr David Lake, of *Enjoy Emotional Freedom, New Energy Therapies,* and *Provocative Energy Techniques: The Manual,* and is also co-author, with Jo Wiese, of *Rose and the Night Monsters,* a children's book on tapping.

Steve's material is grounded in universal principles of success combined with the latest findings of psychology. He uses and teaches practical techniques and strategies you can apply immediately to get better results - with less stress!

If you would like to bring Steve into your company, or benefit from his programs personally, you'll find more information at these websites:

www.eftdownunder.com
www.stevewells.com.au

Made in the USA
Lexington, KY
06 September 2016